TIME AND PHILOSOPHY

TIME AND PHILOSOPHY

Johan Mekkes

Dordt College Press

Cover design by Scott Vande Kraats
Layout by Carla Goslinga

Printed in the United States of America.

Dordt College Press   www.dordt.edu/dordt_press
498 Fourth Avenue NE
Sioux Center, Iowa 51250
United States of America

ISBN: 978-0-932914-92-7

Library of Congress Cataloging-in-Publication Data

Mekkes, J. P. A.
  [Temps. English]
  Time and philosophy / John Mekkes.
    p. cm.
  ISBN 978-0-932914-92-7 (pbk. : alk. paper)
  1. Time. 2. Time--Religious aspects--Christianity. I. Mekkes, J. P. A.
    Tijd der bezinning. English. II. Title.
  BD638.M45 2012
  115--dc23
                         2012012536

Translator's preface

This book contains two different texts written by J.P.A. Mekkes. "Time" first appeared as "Le Temps" in *Philosophy and Christianity* (1965). "Time for Reflection" appeared in 1973 as *Tijd der Bezinning* (Amsterdam: Buijten en Schipperheijn). Both texts can be regarded as summaries of the studies that Mekkes wrote during his career as professor of philosophy at Leiden University: *Scheppingsopenbaring en Wijsbegeerte* (1961) (*Creation, Revelation, and Philosophy*, Dordt College Press, 2010), *Teken en Motief der Creatuur* [Code and Motive of Creation] (1965), and *Radix, Tijd en Kennen* [Radix, Time, and Knowing] (1971). In these studies, Mekkes plumbs the depths of contemporary philosophy. What is the deepest spirit that drives the philosophies of Jaspers, Heidegger, and Sartre? And how are we to understand theological horizontalism?

Remarkably, while Mekkes is of the opinion that "horizontalism" has to be rejected, true christian spirituality does not mean "verticalism." Rather, as "earthly" beings we are called to follow "the Master" in a love that does not escape into an "other world," but that is faithful to the calling of mankind in time.

This highly original thesis of what had come to be known as the "Philosophy of the Cosmonomic Idea" has not always been correctly understood. For life and thought to find basic meaning again, Mekkes therefore critically sets forth the spiritual basics of christian philosophy, for it is the christian reformation of our basic conceptuality that is highly urgent, even today.

I want to thank Bruce C. Wearne for his invaluable assistance with my English. And last but not least, John H. Kok should be mentioned. He had a final, critical look at many points of my translation.

Chris van Haeften, January 2012

TABLE OF CONTENTS

Time

1. Aristotle, Bergson, Einstein 1
2. Philosophy of existence 4
3. A choice to be made 7
4. Modal entry? 11
5. Root and choice 12
6. Universal time 15
7. Givenness 17
8. History and anticipation 21
9. Measuring history 24
10. History's horizon 26
11. Fire 28

Time for Reflection

1. Introduction 31
2. Simple philosophy, useful systematics 31
3. Basic encounter 33
4. Historically concrete philosophizing 35
5. Philosophy and groundmotive 37
6. Boundary area 39
7. Antithesis 41
8. Vantage point? 43
9. Choice of direction 45
10. Archimedean point? 47
11. Motivations 50
12. Sovereign motivation and human history 54
13. Focal point of application 56
14. Developing the "transcendental critique" 58
15. Knowing 62
16. Norm, time, and structure 66
17. Creational dynamics vs. present thinking 70
18. Dynamics, knowing, direction 77
19. Root and thought 82
20. A priori knowing and structural knowing 83

TIME

1. Aristotle, Einstein, Bergson

Is it still possible to say anything of importance with regard to the question of time? Time seems to present itself as a problem, because while man believes that he can make use of nature and its time, he nevertheless cannot avoid passing along with it. The West, from its most ancient philosophers right up until the most recent physicists, has scrutinized time in all possible ways. The difficulties surrounding it have proved to be real, and the more that mortal man was overwhelmed by them, the more they proved to be beyond resolution.

This need not surprise us. The origin of our existence as such is silent before every attempt to defy its inalienable prerogative. The difficulties about time stem from this same root. We are immersed in what we call "time." But we continue to be haunted by the question of the meaning of this dynamic force that drags us along with all that we are, towards a destination that is forever unknown.

Already at this point a choice has to be made. Is time actually a *fundamental* dynamism? Isn't time really the number and measure of movement?[1] Isn't it the expression of a natural power to be controlled, and that, in essence, is being conquered by the profoundly reasonable principle of form? For the scientist this conception of Aristotle's seems to capture a considerable portion of the reality under examination. How could we even begin to understand the meaning of energy, of mass, of velocity, if we could not make use of this concept of time?

However, Einstein's theory has undermined this approach by contesting the absolute value of such a "measure." We do not have to judge about the possible value of either Aristotle's or Einstein's measures for physics. But by taking the speed of light for the measurement of cosmic

---

1   Cf. Aristotle's definition of time: "Time is the number of movement in respect of before and after," *Physics*, IV, 11 (tr).

This essay was originally published in French as "Le Temps" in *Philosophy and Christianity*, Amsterdam, 1965, 31-56. Where Mekkes left a simple blank line in his text to indicate its subdivisions, numbers and titles have been added by the translator.

speeds and distances, Einstein has drawn our attention to a fundamental point, namely that the measure itself of a movement cannot be anything but, once again, a movement. Einstein merely wanted to approach the absolute measure with maximal precision, while this absolute measure, as such, remains beyond the reach of the created mind.

Aristotle had not been able to see this inconvenience. For him the changes among natural bodies derive their movements from the metaphysical principle of contingent matter, while this principle, according to the religious²conception of the Greek philosopher, is as such irreconcilably opposed to the principle of substantial form.

When St. Thomas Aquinas set himself to explain the intentions of Aristotle more exactly, he could not locate the idea that would unify the changes during such movements. As concerns their relations in space and time, the definition of corporeal substantial bodies knew of no other unity, that is to say, of no other reality (*ens et unum convertuntur*³) than the static form of each of them. According to the universal order of reason their meaning was in all respects defined by this static form. Consequently, St. Thomas sought to anchor a reasonable unity of *states* of change *in the very thought of man,* which is flagrantly at odds with the Aristotelian idea of substance. According to Aristotle, substance is in reality independent of human cognition and human sensibility.

But in St. Thomas's conception, movement as well as time, which is supposed to be its number and measure, are bestowed with a synthetic, rather than a realistic concept of unity. The successive states of things during their changes are gathered under a unity of "becoming," and their "numbers" (of before and after) classified in a unitary way under "time," in which the present is conceived in its double relation to and between past and future.

There is certainly a great distance between the old idea of Aristotle and the modern conceptions of time as they have been formulated by Newton, Kant, and Einstein. Under the influence of the progress of natural science and greatly stimulated by the religious pragmatism of our times, principles of method have gained the upper hand over the so-called metaphysical ideas. The only concern now is how some of these

---

2 The meaning of "religion" in use in this article is quite different from how it is usually defined. Mekkes means to indicate all searching for basic meaning. It is to be noticed that he considers a search for such meaning in any so-called supernatural sense to be meaningless (see, e.g., *Creation, Revelation, and Philosophy*, Sioux Center: Dordt College Press, 2010, page 72) (tr).

3 Entity and unity amount to the same (tr).

originally philosophical ideas can be made pragmatically useful for modern positivism.

But the idea of time is not touched by the variations it has had to endure. From its side, so to speak, time is not concerned with the way it is being used to "measure" cosmic velocities, whether great or small. *We* are the ones who cannot but distinguish between the grand and the minute in the regions of the cosmos, but what is it that we really know in this regard? The divergence between Newton's ideas of absolute time and space and Einstein's idea of cosmic expansion is enormous. Measurement seems to have lost all meaning.

We are not going to follow here those admirable thinkers in their physical or metaphysical investigations. Neither are we going to investigate what Bergson has brought to light under the psychological aspect of time as "duration." But we should in no way neglect the remarkable fact that those who have spoken about time under such different aspects have each been right in their own way. Bergson's conception cannot be put aside by mathematicism, but when Aristotle speaks of time's measure as the "number of time according to before and after," it is the three last words that count. For even the *feeling* of time in its psychological sense of spontaneous intuition is inevitably accompanied by an awareness of succession in the "duration."

What, then, is the meaning of the term "number"? We have seen that it cannot suggest anything but another duration, namely the duration of a movement from one point of geometrical space to another. Of which time are we speaking? Apparently it is time in the sense of a physical movement. Also, it is a time that can only be measured in terms of another movement, however regular it may be. And lastly, the special significance of the latter depends on the subject who makes use of it and who sets up his instruments as measures of a second degree. The measures that are in such a way interwoven with each other can never be detached, neither from their actual reality, which is itself only movement, nor from the subject. They can never represent an absolute value, and this is what Einstein has taught us about time, once and for all.

So far we have been speaking about physical time. We have touched on the tension between the traditional opinion with its mathematical tendency and Bergson's conception, which has been judged to be purely subjective. On the other hand, the exact nature that the physicists thought they could claim for their basic measure showed itself to be obtained solely by way of abstraction. Is it correct to reproach Bergson for subjectivism? Isn't it rather as if everything has become uncertain? Without doubt that is how it is if we believe that we can comprehend where we are facing the Divine secret and where thinking itself is encompassed by what it wanted to control.

2. Philosophy of existence

Why should we be surprised that man's thinking is before all else occupied with the time of nature? Man knows himself to be completely dependent on nature. It is nature that makes him live and die; it is nature that compels him to care for and protect his body; it is nature that instructs him about what promotes or what diminishes his vitality. Nature supplies the means for time's measurement: the sun, the moon, the stars, and the change of seasons and of generations. When the "nature" of man—his body—perishes he is no more. He has disappeared from the world, and the world has disappeared for him. But after Western man had overcome his mythological insanity, he has strained all his energy in an unparalleled passion to "overcome" nature. While the philosophers of antiquity had a relative respect for nature and sought some consolation for man's natural fragility in the principle of rational order, humanism is forced to comprehend and to control it. It has achieved great successes. Western culture is drawn more and more into this direction, while the nations that up until now have hardly benefitted from the "blessings" of science and technology stretch out their eager hands towards the products and the instructions of Western intelligence.

In order to examine and control nature there is no need for an *idea* of time. It is replaced by a *concept* of physical time that fits the method for the examination of nature. If it does not lead to the proposed end, it will be replaced by another concept. The old metaphysical question "What is time?"—irritating but without an answer—is no longer asked.

By contrast, the question is increasingly raised from the other side within the humanist world. Existentialism is today the sole philosophy left to raise the question of a possible meaning, however weak, of the bare freedom of our existence. The opposition between the pragmatistic and positivistic tendencies on the one hand and the speculative philosophy of existence on the other hand, show the religious—that is to say, fundamental—polarity that has characterized humanism ever since its origins. It stimulated its philosophical development even as it has pushed this development towards an insurmountable crisis.

While in the past the philosophers engaged each other in a dialectic that bound them together, nowadays we cannot but observe a real and definitive separation between them. For the modern positivists the question of meaning is devoid of any sense. The philosophy of existence, on the other hand, fights by means of a deepened logic in order to defend the last remnants of the idea of human freedom and of meaning, remnants that often amount to a confession of non-meaning. The two original poles of humanist thinking are isolated from each other, the one in the world of pragmatism, the other in the various philosophies of existence. It is nowadays impossible to predict what the next period will bring if not a continued progress of pragmatism.[4]

It does not matter much for our problem. The positivistic methodologies will continue to produce and to use the concepts of time that the physical sciences and the other sciences in their trail will need. But if Western philosophy, philosophy in the true sense of the word, is bound to disappear, then existentialism will have rendered it a last great service by its criticism. In spite of itself, it has shown the abysmal depth of a dialectic without end that ruins thinking itself.

Drawing on the irrational core of the ideas of Søren Kierkegaard for the fertilization of the historicism of Wilhelm Dilthey and the phenomenology of Edmund Husserl and Max Scheler, the philosophy of existence has made us understand the impossibility of a concept of *what is* unless we start with the meaning of the being of the "*subject.*" That subject today is no longer the subject of pure or practical reason as Kant conceived it, nor is it the living subject of Bergson, nor even the subject of history as represented by humanity in Dilthey's account. It is the free, solitary subject of the responsible choice, by which meaning is attributed to being. Humanism has always presented its "subject" as the legislator of meaning, that is to say, as the not-subjected subject. When Sartre says that being (*il y a*) leaps up with the for-itself (*pour soi*, the subject), he says nothing basically new within the Western world. The only difference is that in the preceding philosophies this subject-legislator started by creating the rational order of the *totality*, the universal rational order to which this "legislator" itself would be subject. It is true that this conception of

---

4 See Johan van der Hoeven, *The Rise and Development of the Phenomenological Movement*, Christian Perspectives, 1965, Hamilton, Ontario, p. 16: "Many philosophers, strongly divergent among themselves, who, travelling along different ways, almost all came to an impasse and, more than once inclined to defeatism, clung to 'the' phenomenology as the new perspective. Since this perspective appears to fail as the final insight, for the once enthroned philosophy only two ways seem to be left. On the one hand: an escape into explicit mythology. On the other: the seal of stagnation and of powerlessness in the pragmatistic proclamation of the 'plurality of the truth.' In this case for practical philosophizing there is hardly another avenue left than that of a logicistic thought-and-language technique—*without much to say*" (tr).

order became more and more dynamic with the growth of the idea of human autonomy, but even then the aim remained to develop before all else the view of the totality of *what is*. The idea of time was taken to be inherent in this or that aspect. But from that moment on when the totality of reality was subsumed under the dominant idea of the historical human subject, the idea of time appeared under the denominator of the succession of human actions and the events resulting from them. After Dilthey this denominator lost any element of progression and of universal rationality. For existentialism the choice of the free man is the ever momentary legislator of "meaning," while the conscience that accompanies it is man's "responsibility."

We shall not be concerned here with the details of the philosophies of Heidegger, Merleau-Ponty, or Sartre, all of which hesitantly but inevitably capitulate before the demands of the immanent polarity of which we spoke above. What we are concerned with here is the common idea of time in these philosophies.

Insofar as European philosophy has not completely surrendered to the positivistic and logistic methods of religious pragmatism, the philosophy of existence has forever shifted the emphasis towards subjectivity, deciding, and acting in its temporal "present."

The "present" is the truly original source of decision. In the present, the actual occasion of authentic responsibility, contingent history takes its starting point time and again. We find ourselves thrown into the present, coming from the past, and limited in our choices for the future. It is in the present moment that man is revealed to himself as "existence." As we shall see in the next section, the indivisible moment of the present is indeed spoken of as a moment that reveals what is eternal.

Above we spoke about an abyss that opens itself under the existentialistic criticism. It is not the abyss of "non-being" that is being discussed in these philosophies themselves. Rather, it is the abyss of an insoluble antinomy. As we have seen, the philosophy of existence blames its predecessors for a lack of critical spirit. They had not seen, it says, that the sole archimedean point from which a philosophy can start is to be sought in the existence of the free subject facing its "world." But today the philosophy of existence finds itself threatened by a contradictory dualism that is truly irreconcilable. For the philosopher himself remains an "existence" who "passes" with time, that is to say, with his "present," just like all the other "subjects." Nevertheless, he must present his philosophy with a claim of eternal and universal reason. Covertly the philosopher's reflection is exempted from the universal contingency that the philosophy of existence attributes to all that exists and to every human act in particular. That is why the proud term "risk" does not hold water. Existentialistic philosophy does not risk anything because it wants to retain at all cost its trust in the universality of reason as the only source of truth. This is the abyss into which humanist thinking, at the end of its inevitable development, has tumbled. The *unique* freedom of man who decides "for himself" (*pour soi*) and the *universality* of human reason, whose grace alone he believes to be the source of truth that he must follow, forever exclude each other. This is the abyss where human reason as revelatory of truth runs aground, even by the development of its own and appropriate spirit of criticism.

3.   A choice to be made

Taking account of this "abyss," one needs to note the importance that non-positivistic modern philosophy has ascribed to the historical subject and to the "present" of its time. As Karl Jaspers, that most serious of philosophers, with an ardent desire for truth, writes: "All that appears, all that is known, and all that is aimed for, the past as well as the future, becomes a dimension of everything that is ever historically present. As language of eternity it belongs to the present as such."[5]

Here we no longer find ourselves in the atmosphere of the "objects" of technical science and of the supposedly mathematical time, but in the domain of man as such; of man who is free, but is bound to choose, to be "responsible," in order to act. And for ourselves too, even though for different reasons than for Jaspers, we understand that it is inevitable that we make a choice. And will our choice be for or against either of the philosophical tendencies that we have discussed?

As we indicated, the specialists who claim a concept of time that is valid for their specific science are within their right to do so. But we have to reject all exclusive pretensions that want to impose their proper point of view upon everything else, while at most recognizing the concepts of the others as analogies. This tendency, resulting from the dominant methods of physics in positivist philosophy, threaten to completely obscure the horizon of Western thinking.

On the other hand, the question can be asked if there is not a similar exclusivism on the side of the philosophies that in some way still oppose

---

5   "Alles Erscheinende, alles Gewußte und Bezweckte, das Vergangene und das Zukünftige wird Dimension des jeweils geschichtlich Gegenwärtigen als Sprache der Ewigkeit. Zur Gegenwart selbst gehört es als sie selbst." *Von der Wahrheit,* Darmstadt, 1983, 173.

the pragmatistic tendencies. Do the philosophers of history accept the validity of the concept of physical time?

It is more than that. It is not just that they do accept its validity. For a large sector of them, and in particular for the logicians among the existentialists, their dialectics fasten upon the data that natural science and mathematical abstractions put at their disposal without yet succeeding in their logic to solve the riddle. They leave to the sciences all their value, including their concepts of time. But, according to the philosophers of existence, it is another time that is decisive. It is the time of responsible man, time with its exstases,[6] the time of man's *freedom*. The logicians of history and existence, and the latest philosopher of "meaning" (*sens*)[7] take the dynamics of this decisive time as the basis for their dialectical logic.

The "present," which we have already mentioned and in which the other two exstases meet, is the present of the free choice, the origin of meaning. That is why Jaspers talks about the historical present as the voice of eternity. In the supreme moment existence decides in the face of "transcendence," knowing itself to be given to itself by that which transcends it. Strict individuality and universality, solitary decision and universal validity, contingency and reason come together in that moment of decision.

Thinking about the choice to be made, the question urges itself upon us: Where shall we start in order to approach the idea of time? Should we base our investigations on the mathematically defined "measures"? But we have seen that that leads to an infinite regress, from measure to measure, because both motion and space persist in their own proper meaning. The question is about meaning, with its mysterious modalities. What is its origin: how do we find an entry to it? Isn't that the question we have to ask before we decide?

In preparing ourselves for this choice about meaning, we do well to remember that within the world of humanism a philosophy like that put forward by Karl Jaspers is opposed to positivism. His idea of time, concentrated in the eternity of the "present," is the supreme expression of modern man's sovereign freedom. It is fundamentally—at the religious base of humanism—opposed to the basic *a priori* of positivism, namely the idea of the intellectual omnipotence of the possible scientific methods. There is a fundamental religious polarity between these two poles. They mutually presuppose and exclude each other.

Positivism from the outset excludes each and every idea that does

---

6   Exstases: Heidegger calls past, present, and future the *Ekstasen* of time (tr).

7   M. Merleau-Ponty, *Sens et Non-sens*, 1948 (tr).

not yield a concept of time that is all ready for use and verifiable by its "methods." It does not recognize any reality of meaning, nor any meaning of reality, outside of the limits of its methods. As concerns "time," it can only work by analogy with "undisputed" analogies.

If we do not want to bow under the yoke of measures-without-end, should we then not enter by way of the "subject"? Do we not feel in ourselves some faint assent when we read the later Heidegger? Isn't it true that man should take heed that he listens to the voice of being as the voice of meaning? And has not Jaspers told us the same truth, when he proposed to us his idea of transcendence? So, our question has to be: What is the meaning of the idea of transcendence that he puts forward?

For Jaspers it is the *idea* of meaningfulness. He presents it as an idea of his faith, his supreme and final idea, just about divine but, as he confesses, a philosophical faith, a faith upheld by reason. Only by a direct confrontation with this transcendence does "existing" man come to know himself. Awareness of meaning, and obedience to meaning, only enter into the world via the entrance of this faith.

Jaspers is right: faith is confidence; it is ultimate trust. For him it is trust in reason, and as such a mere human affair (humanism!). Jaspers made no secret of it, while Heidegger affirmed it in his own way. The existentialist logicians, even though reasoning along different lines, have anchored their ultimate trust in logic. Logic is for them the guarantee of the validity of reason itself (so much so, that often the purport of their idea of mere existence is hardly to be distinguished from how they describe positivism).

Why this confidence in reason? How can it be maintained at the rim of the abyss where thought strands in the antinomy between the unique existence of the philosopher and the universal validity of his philosophical reflection, between the refusal to consider any idea of meaning and the uncritical surrender to positivistic and logicistic thought as sole valid meaning? The way Jaspers explains this for himself is as surprising as it is sincere: "All that the individual can do, is express the logic of his faith, as I am trying to do in this book."[8]

While positivism knows of no confession, Jaspers presents his faith as a *unique* confession of a *universal* reason. In either case there is the reality of faith as there is no man without an ultimate commitment. Man can refuse to recognize it, or he can recognize it and express it. But he

---

8   "Der Einzelne kann nur die Denkungsart seines Glaubens aussprechen, wie ich es in diesem Buch versuche." *Der philosophische Glaube angesichts der Offenbarung*, Darmstadt 1983, p. 500.

cannot explain it. It is beyond explanation. How would it be possible to explain ultimate confidence? Rather, it is faith that explains the manner of thought. Faith drives and directs all of life, our thinking included.

From a philosophical point of view one cannot reproach anyone who, for his philosophical thinking, places his trust in "human reason." However, what is legitimately reprehensible is that he tries to disavow this ultimate commitment as being a commitment of confidence and faith.[9] Even Karl Jaspers, who talks so openly about his "philosophical faith," has silently let the fact pass by that, in his book about reason and existence, he claims *universal* acceptance for his ideas because of a reason that in the final instance unites all "thinkers." We are faced here with reason as the judge in its own cause.

There is no escape for human reason that wants to keep the last word to itself. As the final instance of resort it is victory or defeat; there is no possibility of an ulterior "reasonable" decision.

In reason as the highest authority, we meet, first, with the whole tradition of the West from antiquity up until our own days. Secondly, it contains the high pretension of human rationality, judging itself to be the sole instance capable of bringing about radical and integral truth.

Will it be possible for us to choose between the two poles of present-day humanism? It would be nothing but a choice between reason and professional logic, which would amount to nothing more than a choice between the shades of one and the same polarity. As we saw, it is the polarity between, on the one hand, the rule of method and, on the other hand, human thinking insofar as it leaves the methods of physics behind to investigate the human subject. According to the explanation given us by Jaspers, it is reason (*Vernunft*) that takes understanding (*Verstand*) into its service. But in reality this means that it is man's intellect that decides both about measures and norms, about the measures to be used in the sciences of nature, as well as about the "metaphysics" of freedom. At the same time it is the idea of "freedom," feeble as it is, that has to hold the tension between existentialist philosophy and positivism in place. In vain it tries to build a barrier against the threats posed by the consequences of logic.

---

9 | Why does the believer in reason not show the basis of his belief? What is the structural cause of his fundamental dissimulation of the fact that he believes in reason? It can only be sought in the structural meaning of faith itself. It is not there to look at itself, but, according to its norm, at Him in whom man *ought* to trust.

4.   Modal entry?

We had to interrogate the choice offered by the religious dialectic of humanism. We discovered its hidden or open pretensions of autonomy. And it appears that it is impossible for us to accept the choice that it bequeaths to us.

For what was it talking about? What has Western philosophy been talking about ever since its beginning? What else but our existence and all its concerns?! But then, what is the fundamental nature of our earthly existence?

If for an answer to this question we have to reject a dialectic that gets itself entangled in the contradictions of its ambitions and its faith, then where shall we search if not in the Word of humility and hope? Its humility is true to life. For when man comes into the world, he starts to interrogate *reality given* to him. And what is a given reality but a sovereign revelation?

Sovereign revelation is at odds with the pretensions of autonomy. The end of existence is not merely the impossibility of all possibles. It is as such the condemnation of any authoritarian logic.

Let this be well understood. In no way would we deny the proper laws of logic as a mode of our existence and as a real modality of the cosmos. That is impossible. When a man thinks, he *makes use* of his logical mode, his intellectual function—here we agree in a certain sense with Jaspers. But in his *act* of thinking, like in all his other acts, he *equally* makes use of all his other modal functions. Acts are actual acts of activity; they are actual because of the cosmic dynamism that generates them and by which man opens and directs all potentialities of creation. The act of thinking too, that powerful motor of Western civilization, transcends on all sides that which we, by way of abstraction, call the intellect. The act of thinking is completely comprised by time's dynamics.

In this way we get to the problem of time via the gate of man, man acting and responsible for all his acts, that is to say, the subject in the true sense of the word. Not the subject who presents himself as legislator of his history, nor the subject who hides behind the imperious acts of his positivistic science. Rather, it is the subject who, with all his thinking, knows himself to be moved by the powerful dynamism of revelatory creation, where, before all else, we meet time that carries us along.

Positivism has branded its counter-pole a metaphysics, because it talks about the human subject that as such cannot be the "object" of the mathematical or physical sciences, nor of a so-called exact logic. As we have shown, we in no way accept the "metaphysics" of present-day humanists, but we would like to know whether the demand of the analytical school, according to which truth must be "verifiable," is itself able to escape from metaphysics as long as it has not verified this demand itself.

Very plausibly man will be spontaneously interested in the natural modalities of time as they regulate life and death. And what is more, the natural sciences are able to push their abstractions almost just as far as they deem useful. In that way they can play with the idea of time as much as they need to in order to serve the continuity of human civilization. They can do all that, but only on the condition that they do not transgress the boundaries of their competence and that they do not impose their concept of time as an idea of totality, nor impose their abstractions as if they are concrete reality.

The same is true for a philosophy of the "subject." For this subject is not the same as man in the totality of his existence. What is called "existence" does not go beyond one modality of man either; it does not reach further than his modality of "history," taken in the existentialistic sense. As we have seen, in this idea of history we meet the "historical moment," the "present" of decision. The philosophy of existence has refashioned the old "cogito," the subject of actual logical consciousness, by giving her a new set of clothes, the modality of "existence."

According to existentialism, man projects himself, in some way or other, towards the end of his journey by living his history in the dialectic of his "presents." Everything is construed here around this dialectical center: temporality, historicity, the class struggle, the meaning of corporality and of language, the structures of being, the hypostatization of some supposed transcendence and of some reason that searches to listen to the voice from the depths or to establish the communication between human existents, etcetera, etcetera. Yet, the common denominator is but this conscious dialectic, projecting contingent history along the flow of time. This time, with its exstases[10] of past, present and future, is the time of the individual subject.

But if man equally transcends all the modalities of his earthly presence, then the entry to the problem of time via the gate of man will never succeed by partaking in the dialectic of the modalities, even if it be the dialectic of a historicistic philosophy or the profound religious dialectic between it and the pragmatists of our day.

5.   Root and choice

It is impossible to find a foothold in one of the modalities of our

---

10 See note 6.

"temporal" existence, since each of them—thinking included, whatever it be called—finds itself on all sides engulfed and carried along by time. Where then shall we start to tackle its "problem"?

Should we call it a problem? Does it in any way allow for a solution? Certainly not, as long as we foster the illusion that we can form a precise concept of it, or even a speculative idea.

The Christian is obliged to confront the fundamental ideas of the civilization through which it has pleased God to call and to guide him in order that he would understand the witness that the Master demands from him. Willingly, often too willingly, he accepts what the wisdom of past centuries and the science of his day want to teach. But he will not be able to escape from a permanent examination of the ultimate profound basics of what has been spelled out by the sages of tradition.

Then it will become ever more clear to him that in these basics—which his philosophy must bring to light—man has reserved the first and the last word of truth for himself, for his intellect as such, that is to say, for his autonomous intellect. Consciously or unconsciously, in an open or an implicit dialectic, man reserves this prerogative for himself, with open and studied contradictions or, for that matter, with suppressed and dissimulated contradictions; at base all such contradictions are, after all, religious in nature.

This "last word" illegitimately takes the role of revelation, occupying the place of Him from whom all things originate and who alone has the right to speak first.

Without a doubt, man speaks of realities that present themselves to him. But knowing them depends on knowing their root, the same root from which the act of knowing itself originates. We therefore have to continue our critical investigation, seeking to probe the ultimate background where traditional wisdom took its origin.

This critical struggle demands a chivalrous attitude from the Christian. Nevertheless, it goes all the way up to the ultimate limits of all intellectual possibilities, to end up in a final confrontation of these same possibilities. It will lay bare that a radical decision by a thinking that takes itself to be autonomous is ultimately impossible. The disarray of the fundamental dialectic that we spoke about is the manifestation of this impossibility.

It goes without saying that the "adversary" will not accept the norms of this final critique. The dialectics that we criticize is for him the ultimate wisdom. And because there will no longer be an earthly judge, the adherents of the religious dualism of "nature and grace" will also object to

13

engage in this struggle according to this design. For them the final word is being reserved for a theological philosophy that even allocates the role and content of Scripture in the overall intellectual conception.

Nevertheless, for the Christian the discovery of this situation can in no case be a reason to choose what could appear to be a new "starting point." He cannot but start from faith.

Man, thinking man as well, lives in his acts. The act of thinking is, like all other acts, a temporal act. That is God's order for the earthly creature, valid "for all times." That means that it is not possible for created man to choose for himself some point outside the flow of time to make judgments about this order. He is comprised by it with his whole life and with all that he does and thinks. Never is he able to find himself outside of the dynamism in the root of his existence, where he is being pushed forward. Neither his understanding of time nor his understanding of his thinking will ever be able to start from a point outside of this evolving current. Nevertheless, it is not time that decides about the *direction* of our lives and of our thinking, as some try to teach us at the end of the twentieth century. This is where we find the great and decisive secret.

We have not only rejected the various denominators under which scientific thought has tried to capture the different modalities of life and by consequence life's time itself. We also have to reject all speculative thinking that shows the same autonomous pretensions. There is no neutral position, nor is it possible to refrain from a decision. Time surrounds us on all sides, and it leaves us no escape for any part of our intellectual activity. It forces us to choose. It forces us to take our position with regard to it, because it pushes us towards the destination of our existence. This choice, as we have understood by now, cannot primarily be a choice of thought. Man's thinking follows his ultimate faith, even if it be the faith in his reason.

Thus, we have to choose. Where shall we place our trust? In human reason? We declined its self-destructive dialectic. From this it follows that we equally reject the dualism of ancient and modern scholasticism. We cannot accept a human word for the final revelatory word.

As the anchor for our confidence we have chosen the Word of humility and hope. For man, inserted in the flow of time, with his intellect and with all that he has and is, there is no other issue. The Word in which we trust is the Word of Him who alone is the Master of time.

Once more, we want to be understood correctly. We have drawn the consequences of our original thesis, and we have *chosen* to express ourselves the way we did. Yet this is not a theological decision. Theology is a science like all the others, and what it brings forward is nothing but the consequence of the radical choice that man cannot avoid making in all that he takes upon himself. There is not more to theory than that this choice works itself out according to the proper nature of theoretical endeavor.

6. Universal time

Only now we are *really* faced with the problem of time and all its deep implications. If every act of our life is based on an open or hidden original choice, then what is time's order of choice? Does man first make (or repeat) his original choice and only thereafter "subsequently" acts? It goes without saying that "number and measure of movement" does not apply here. But neither does the historical succession apply, neither in the idealistic, nor in the existentialistic sense.

No, existentialism does not clarify the order of succession here either. For existence proceeds from "present" to "present." That is to say, from choice to choice, in face of the possibilities of the situations that present themselves successively without end. Sartre may warn us that human reality cannot be resolved into a succession of "instantaneous" existences, since then the past instant would be *present* as contingent *past*.[11] But it is clear that he nevertheless maintains such a "reality" for the sake of the only reality he is able to discern, namely that of his own dialectic.

What is the time of choice that decides all our choices? It is not natural time, nor is it historical time; although neither of them, nor any of the other modalities, can be eliminated from universal time.

It is universal time![12] It is neither a modality nor the sum total of its modalities. The modal conception of time, that we again and again had to reject as being invalid, has been the cause of so much philosophical confusion in antiquity and of even more confusion in the period of humanistic philosophy. But it is from universal time that all specific experience of its majestic currents derives. How shall we discuss it if all our speaking and all our understanding is penetrated by its powerful dynamism?

Surely, we can to a certain degree understand what Karl Jaspers meant when he spoke of the historical present as the voice of eternity. This vision was inspired by his idea of transcendence as a philosophical synthesis between rational universality and existential freedom. But, as we have seen, his idea of transcendence was paralyzed from the bottom

---

11 E.g., Sartre, *L'être et le néant*, pages 195–96.

12 Dooyeweerd: cosmic time (tr).

up by the involuntary dialectic between the existence of the philosopher, contingent in all that he chooses, and the universal and exclusive validity of the philosophy chosen by him. In other words, Jaspers' idea of the union between eternity and contingent existence in the "present" moment is but an expression of this original paralysis. It will never be able to direct our attention towards a transcendence that is truly eternal. Yet, the choice that will be truly original has to be an original response to "the voice of eternity." There is some original "union" here.

The Christian must demand from every man of science that he "confesses" his inevitable a priori instead of hiding it for himself and for his fellow scientist. And for his part, he must clear up the primary philosophical problem that presents itself here if he is to arrive at an open solution even though it will not be unanimously accepted. When this is how things stand, then he must declare what that means: the union of eternity[13] and my original choice. And his confession must be an expression of what is *valid* for all.

Karl Jaspers, too, declared himself publicly. But he had to take recourse to an idea of "transcendence" in which he hypostasized a subjectivity and a rationality that were both equally final. Thus for Jaspers transcendence is a transcendence "from below," a limit of thought. He declared it to be the source of all human autonomy, both existentially as well as rationally. But, as such, he thought that transcendence to be *unattainable* for the concretely "existing" *philosopher.*

By contrast, the transcendence to which the Christian knows himself to be subject does not allow for any idea of an original human autonomy. It is not at the disposal of our philosophy nor of our theology. It is the truth beneath all opinions and all intellect, even though it is not beyond our understanding. It leaves no other option but to yield or to revolt. The voice of eternity that *should be obeyed* is the voice of the God of Jesus Christ.

The union between eternity and human existence is an *original* unity. By consequence it is a union of love and obedience. It is original, while "without him was not anything made that was made" (John 1:3). And it is a union of love and obedience, because "to all those who received him, he gave the power to become children of God" (John 1:12).

This response is the recognition of *what is.* Our time, the time of creation, rests on the eternity of Him who is the beginning and the end and who does not leave room for us to form a judgment from the outside about what this time *is.* There *is no* autonomous intellect, outside of time.

---

13 It is to be remembered that in French God JHWH is referred to as *L' Éternel* (tr).

In reality man's intellect can only function on the basis of faith. The faith that God commands finds the time of creation to be the dynamic trajectory of the creating and liberating Spirit (Romans 8). It is the trajectory by which the entire creation marches towards its "eternal" destination.

We have to live the different modalities of time with our gaze fixed on eternity, where the secret of time is kept in store. Of this "eternity" we *know only* what holy Scripture tells us, and that is very little. Scripture tells us about the Eternal One and of his love. Our thinking, raising itself respectfully towards Him, has no competence here whatsoever, if it is not a thinking full of love and trust. Scholastic thinking, often balancing between its autonomous pretensions, some of which it was hardly conscious of, does not help us in the least, just as little as any gnostic mysticism will do. We are only to adore the Eternal One without comprehending anything about His "eternity." By starting from *His* creating eternity we find ourselves in the midst of the mysterious current of time. It belongs to Him, and it is being directed by Him.

We find ourselves in the midst of this stream and we look around for something to hold on to: Where do we find a starting point from which we can start to approach the eternal King and his creation, ourselves included?

7. Givenness

What a poverty is demonstrated by positivism, and by the christian thinkers who, in its wake, believe that they can follow its methods and its concepts of time without demur! How is it possible to miss the great mystery we are privileged to watch and to suppose that we can form an exact concept of it? How dare we continue with our abstractions, supposing that that from which we abstract makes no difference for our special science, or even that the idea of time itself specifically depends upon this same special science?

Nevertheless, many of our physicists reject a priori that their doctrines of time have any relation to the secret that we meet in it. That is because surreptitiously their "measures" of time sneak in among the realities that they pretend to measure. For the rest of human life they only allow that we speak of "time" as analogous to their doctrines. They thereby make a fatal mistake!

It is true; the passing of our lives is measured by atomic and solar circulations, and the possibilities of our thinking and feeling change "at the same time" as we grow older. Our age and its possibilities "depend" to some degree upon the "number" of our years. But is this to say that the meaning of this life itself *depends upon* what we can measure in this way, or possibly even on this measure itself? If not, dare we maintain that the structures of the cosmos are independent of the meaning of human life?

If, as Christians, we dare not, then there can be no doubt about the sense of the dependence here. Positivism will be impossible once for all. The groanings of creation (Romans 8) wipe it out. The christian philosopher, instead of following positivism from afar, is theoretically bound to expose its antinomies and to replace them by a structural analysis of the relations between the modalities of time.

The various modalities of our life's time impose their reality upon our practical and theoretical attention. But where shall we start our investigation of them? It would be tempting to have a go with a method of superposition[14] as suggested by the doctrine of "common grace." The latter has greatly stimulated our understanding of created relations. However, it is a doctrine that suffers from the dualism of nature and grace. Even in antiquity philosophers paid attention to some apparent lower-and-higher in things or aspects of the cosmos. This continued into the twentieth century. The idea of such a dualistic architectonics was to an important degree supported by the evolutionistic hypothesis of Darwin. It has even, in spite of his deepest intentions, influenced Karl Jaspers in his thesis of the rupture of being (*Zerrissenheit des Seins*).

Surely, the different domains of entities—physical, biological, psychic—and the reality of human existence with its many and variegated norms, which from moment to moment force us to choose, are easily recognized. But we have to take into account that recognizing the clearly given reality of this variegated givenness is one thing, while the investigation of the "modalities" of creation is quite another. We already touched on the fact that initially the discovery of the given modalities led to a confusion of entities with modalities. The modalities became the denominator for the understanding of the metaphysical substances with their accidents. Yet, the discovery of the modalities provoked the battle for the purification of the theoretical methods.

In this respect, August Comte's ideas have been more influential than the idea of superposition (layering). He supposed that there is an order of succession and of increasing complexity in the methods applied to the different domains of reality and of human life. He added that each

---

14 The general sense of superposition, placing the one on top of the other, of "layering," is sufficient to understand what Mekkes means here. From the context it appears that he means an understanding of reality in two stories: a "lower" story, nature, and an "upper" story, grace (or the supernatural realm) (tr).

of these methods should be solidly and exactly based upon the method for the less complicated domain preceding it. Starting from the less complicated, there had to be an exact control in the progress of method.

But the struggle about the right method became quite intense. Without embarrassment positivism started the game about the denominators again, admitting no other meaning than the one prescribed by its methodology. It supposed the general method to be that of the sciences of nature.

But this is where the confusion starts. For what is nature? Is it that which biology is concerned with, or is it that other "nature," that of physics, with its mathematical relations? Or is it perhaps the movement of the problematic "particle" with its measures for the subjective approximation of this movement?

Comte brought the complication to light, but at the same time he maintained the methodology of "layering" on the basis of a natural scientific denominator. Today the methods of the sciences have been infinitely refined, yet the overall logic of naturalism, in a broad sense, is being conserved. More and more the successes of the natural sciences have become prescriptive for philosophy rather than being a stimulus for the philosophical spirit of inquiry. For such naturalism, it remained permanently necessary that it could adopt a method analogous to that of the natural sciences.

But, contrary to what was being believed by its adherents, they were no longer speaking of total entities. In fact they were talking about modalities, the very modalities that they had refused to recognize under the restraint of the naturalistic method, but that nevertheless do not let themselves be demeaned. They take revenge, so to speak, even in spite of the blindness of the positivist specialist, because at an unwelcome moment they demand recognition of their proper significance by breaking the reins of the dogmatic denominator. It will never be possible to approach the reality of life by means of physical methods, or the reality of social relations by means of mathematical concepts mixed with some so-called empiricism. We talked about such revenge in §1—thought ends up in insoluble dialectics when subjective thinking is proclaimed to be universal and eternal, while at the same time the reality that encompasses and engulfs the subject is said to be contingent, or even meaningless.

It goes without saying that the real givenness of the diversity of the domains of real entities is not affected by some imperialism of method. And yet the irreducible real givenness of the modal variety is then unfortunately no longer seen. For the recognition of the modalities as given realities not only demands a *real* adaptation of method but, above and before all, also the consistent recognition that these modalities disclose an infinite anticipation. That is why they never yield to an authoritarian method. Their unity cannot be recovered via a synthesis of abstractions. Such unity remains forever abstract. Therefore, the order between the modalities does not allow such superpositioning: that would not overcome the dead abstraction. In concrete reality we will only be able to see this order in the *real* and given entities. The modalities are aspects of *them*, and only in them can the modal order really be seen. But it takes humility to accept the real givenness before dedicating ourselves to theoretical analysis.

It is clear that we are making a confession here. But it is no more a confession than that of autonomous thinking that chooses its various denominators under the dialectical religious reins of humanism. Autonomous thought remains silent about its ultimate confession, be it that of meaning or of non-meaning.

The understanding of the given order, right or false, starts with faith, in its turn true or false. The Word by which everything was made desired it to be so. The human creature can only approach creation, with which it has been entrusted, by knowing its Creator. The way of knowing is not a way of domination; it is a way of humility and obedience.

Here we take up the order of time again. If the Christian is prepared to accept the anticipatory nature of time's dynamics, then he can only start from the root of this power of life and truth. He will not accept any result from the positivistic school without making it take the route of the origin, verifying the "fact" over against each and every basis given by positivism itself.

Neither will he side with the historicistic schools of thought, nor with any modern attempt at a diplomatic conciliation by the philosophy of existence with the Anglo-Saxon schools of thought by means of an "interpretative ontology," and so on. Such tendencies base their fundamental scheme of a conscious subject and a mirroring object upon faith in human autonomy. They change the created dynamism for a dialectic of reason. Such attempts may claim to acknowledge the dynamism of time. But in fact they are no more than the dynamism of reflection reflecting on its reflections. They mask the failure of the revolting religious passion that designs the Creator according to the image of the fleeting human intellect. And they have but one goal: to combat the last remnants of the idea of an order that is *given*.

Christians have possibly taken the philosophy of the world far too seriously and for far too long. We can and should admire the thoughts of the great philosophers of antiquity, who during "the times of ignorance" (Acts 17:30, profound words of the apostle) have sought after the truth. But what shall we think of Western man who has rejected the "invitation" and turned his back on it?

Any pride would be out of place here. The "solidarity" in fall and distress is all too sore and all too real. Nevertheless, there is another solidarity. It does not come from us, nor from our human fellows. It presents itself and it invites us. It warns us in our hearts about the revelations of autonomous thought, under whatever denominator they appear to us. And it instructs us about the meaning of time. By faith!

So, when it is for us to start the philosophical discussion of time, we know where to start. Our view of time can only start from the wholly opened up modality of faith. In faith the anticipatory architectonics of creation is really unleashed. By faith God keeps his creation on the move, as it is focused in the responsibility of man. And creation's direction is none other than that of the *Resurrection*. Its road travels via the cross.

8.   History and anticipation

The christian understanding of time, therefore, is from the outset decided by this cross. Broadly speaking, nonchristian ideas of time either conceive of time as a closed circle from which we can only escape by a leap, or as the horizontal movement of a dialectic that gets nowhere. But the scriptural conception of time is linear, as has been clearly explained by Oscar Cullmann.[15]

It has been objected that Cullmann gives a simple "representation" with too little "theological" attention for God's transcendence, independent of historical time. There must be more to God's transcendence than that the Eternal One chooses his temporal "kairoi"[16] and uses them for directing history, as Cullmann has it.

These feeble reproaches came from Roman Catholic writers. It is not difficult to surmise behind them the scheme of nature and grace that has difficulty identifying the "nature" of the Son of God with that of his "brothers," including their temporality.

But here lies precisely the great secret. In the history of theology, there have been plenty of heresies resulting from "last words" other than that of Scripture. The church has done well to reject them. But a decision

---

15   *Christ and Time* (1946), and *Salvation in History* (1965) (tr.).

16   *Kairos*, pl. *kairoi*, is the Greek word the Bible uses for the occasions of time God pleases to choose to fill them with his glory (tr).

like that is not necessary where Scripture does not leave anything for man to decide. We are subject to the order of time. Therefore it is not possible for us to rise to the level of transcendence in order to form a judgment about the relation between the temporal and the Sovereign's eternity. Or what is it we would want to say about the elevated Christ? What counts is the relation of the holy Creator with his sinful creature. Here Scripture does not leave us in any doubt.

The holy Creator makes his history with us. It is a history of salvation. Man can refuse. He can choose not to put his trust in it. But it does not change by that. Man remains subject to it: "whoever does not believe stands condemned already" (John 3:18). That is why the "faith" of the "unbeliever" directs his life towards the non-meaning of a pretended intellectual autonomy, dialectically returning to its point of departure. Such dialectic is a disruptive force. It has practically dispersed the humanist world into its two poles, and even inside each of them the disruption continues.

By contrast, for him who *does believe,* the cross in the midst of all ages is the only signpost that shows us where to go. For the elevation of our Savior took place on the cross, and by way of the cross. The Christian knows of no leap in order to free himself from a "prison" of time. Rather, with the apostles he has seen the Lord rise to heaven, where it is to be understood that the transcendence of heaven is not the "out there," beyond time, but the Spirit being present with all creation. With "the children of God" creation expects deliverance, not from time, but from corruptibility. From time we need not be delivered. Jesus himself speaks of eternal centuries *(aiones)* without any intention of communicating to us what *aion* means except a duration free from the corruptions of the present times.

That is the anticipatory meaning of creation. Its direction and destination are shown by the glorious elevation of the Son of Man. All that man is, and all that he does, presupposes his faith. Faith proper *should be* the positive response to the invitation to follow creation's destination. The man who accepts launches the struggle with himself and with the world of corruption of which he is a part. It will be a struggle of active testimony in the footsteps of the Master, who acted at the decisive moment. He continues to do so.

But if man refuses the invitation, he will follow the ways of the world. Still, that world will not lose its created nature, and therefore it retains its dynamic architectonics. By consequence, it will chain the lost man in all the practical and theoretical embarrassments of a perplexed existence, even if, most often, it is initially under the appearance of the opposite.

The first thing he will lose sight of will be the "vertical," or transcendental dimension of the order of time. Then he will be enclosed by the circle of a treacherous horizontalistic dialectic. But he will not be able to recognize it. Yet he finds himself pursued by the endless debate within autonomous science about the denominators under which it has to keep the real entities in order to maintain itself. In fact, the reality of the real entities must be left behind to be forgotten, since such science bases its pretensions upon the exchange of their reality for the non-reality of an abstract denominator. The autonomous thinker is being tossed to and fro between the successive and very effective powers of the *world* "of science." The capitulation, within a couple of years, of the existentialist camp before pragmatism is a sign of this. The ingenious diplomacy by which it is accompanied highlights it even more. For humanism, as well as the Christians who have been searching for their fortune with it, tired of their failing "interpretations," that is to say, of a vacuous freedom—the day does not seem far away on which they will surrender body and soul.

For in reality the debate is a combat. It is the struggle for power between men, fought by scientific means for the camouflage of the combatants. Its stakes are high: nothing less than competent control over the whole of life by man. Still, in spite of the camouflage, human actions and their organizations continue to show the transcendental architectonics of time from which one never can escape. To man, God has entrusted time and creation. Everywhere time makes itself felt, and everywhere man encounters the Creator's dynamism: in the time of nature, in the time of life, in the time of history.

Yet, time offers no opening to an understanding of its meaning as long as meaning is being repulsed behind the various theoretical and practical denominators that serve as shelters for one and the same idol of abstract thought. There is only one way to approach the real modalities of meaning: it has to be recognized that they are the diverse aspects of all created entities and that as such they always and everywhere provide a disclosure of the prior anticipatory tendency of a transcendental and revelatory dynamism. It is not "thought" that demands primary attention, but the living *act* of thinking. Together with all that exists, thinking is directed by anticipatory faith. And before we can make abstractions for the sake of science, it is necessary to realize that things and situations are engaged in the full activity of the human act when they become the object of human insight. In this way they are already interpreted in the light of an ultimate confidence. This ultimate faith plays its determining role for scientific interpretation on two consecutive occasions.

It is a mistake when the historian of philosophy presents the development of philosophy as the results of the successive unfolding of a debate of the subject "man" with the object "world." In reality man never finds himself "opposed to" his world. He lives, penetrated by the dynamism of time directed towards eternity and permeated by, and part of, the world surrounding him. Man can accept and follow, or he can refuse and get lost. Theorizing is merely one special activity among all of man's activities. By giving a theoretical account of his multifarious reality, man can be very much enriched, or he can be forever confused.

The fundamental error of science has been that it has put itself and its abstractions in first place. It has mistaken the theoretic correlation between the thinking subject and its object for substantial reality, taking this abstraction as the basis of knowledge and life. Starting from this error it is not possible to discover given reality. Some denominator is instead taken, functionalistically, for real time.

Ever since the beginning of the nineteenth century, both positivism and the various historicisms have been guilty of this basic error. We shall not return to their description. But we must give an explanation of historicism's difficulties in giving a clear account of what "history" is. And we shall have to do this in a way similar to the explanation we have given of the difficulties positivism had with regard to a proper evaluation of the natural aspects of human life and of time.

Time and history are very closely related. But what exactly is the nature of their relatedness? For historicism they are practically identical. That is why it eagerly describes itself as "dynamic" in opposition to the idea of an order of time that is supposed to be "static."

If we do not a priori yield to the pretensions of positivism, it is obvious that there is a "time of history" that is different from the "time of nature." But it is undeniable that we get into pure nonsense if we try to think of a history of time. What could that possibly mean? Nothing, if we had no measures according to which we could qualify and mark the periods and the validity of what we call history.

9. Measuring history

Like all the other terms that are used in theoretical analysis, the word "history" does not arise from a purely theoretical origin. No matter under which aspect we discuss history, everybody understands what we are talking about. Even the idea of "history in general" makes sense.

But this very distinction between "in general" and "under this or that point of view" can tell us something. Man does not make a "history in general." Rather, he is guided by specific and quite different intentions that are at each time induced by the situation in which he finds himself, surrounded by powers that either can support or oppose him. These situations and powers, in turn, came from other preceding intentions, that were present in the world around. They have produced the circumstances of today. Thus the cardinal question remains: What is the origin of our deepest intentions; where ultimately do we want to finish; what is it that we take to be the decisive destination? Apparently, what we need before all else is a point of view for the direction and the goal of our activity.

There have been innumerable and always changing points of view over the centuries. We will not discuss them. We have but to pay attention to two guidelines, and it is in terms of these that we shall have to search in order to understand the *meaning* of history. If we would not succeed in finding both of these guiding points of view, all that would be left to us would be to let "time" pass without any other dimension than the one that results in our death—that is, the time that we measure by means that already depend on the passing of time—the time of physical movements, of the seasons and ages, of occurrences and catastrophes, investigations and dialectics, the time of egoism and pragmatism, the time that is called "history." But history of what? What more would it be than the history "of time," history without a proper measure, history deprived of every sense and direction?

If history is to have meaning—and meaning it has, since what else would make us suffer or hope except this hidden but undeniable sense?—then we have to look for it in everything that passes with time, though it does *not* originate *from* things passing. But this is what has to be rejected by both pragmatistic positivism and the different forms of historicism. For pragmatism, the only possible meaning of time depends on mathematical measures in connection with physical movement; for historicism it is the intrinsically dialectical continuity of all that passes as it is philosophically conceived between the two poles of freedom without a base and the absolute authority of intellectual reason.

This confession of faith in autonomous reason has to be opposed from our side. God has given us modal "points of view" (the "horizontal" line) so that all our intentions, active in history under these given points of view, can realize their true meaning only if they persevere in the direction assigned by the Word of faithful Truth (the "vertical" line). It is that Word that creates meaning.

When we work with these two lines in view, we meet the true measures of history along them. They are the two dimensions of our earthly time. We find the first line (of the modalities) wherever man exercises his interior and exterior activity. Here we meet with the specific meanings of love, right, economy, language, intelligence, etc. They can in no way be reduced to historicity as such. They are opposed to every sort of dialectic that would want to dominate them.

They maintain themselves against historicism because they are anchored on the second (transcendental) line. This line ought to be the integral guideline of human intentions. Disobedience leads to inevitable, even if unrecognized, consequences. But, what is more, this guideline shows us the way of God's inviting love, the way of humble submission to the cross.

To see this connection between divine love and the way of the cross clearly, we should never confuse man's practical behavior with what he has received as God's desire for his action at his particular point in history. That error leads to a theological historicism that strives to replace the analogies of being by analogies of existence between God and man.

10. History's horizon

The idea of the crossroads of the christian conception of time needs further elaboration. The dynamism of creation is being realized by way of God's history with humanity. Time is the trajectory of this dynamism. That is why we can in no way identify history with time.

The temporal routes that man is obliged to follow by the Creator are in a rich variety of ways qualified by the various modalities of time. More concretely, it is the totalities of human activity that are qualified by them. These totalities are dynamic entities. Each of them shows the whole potential of the modal architectonics of creation, each according to its specific modification. During the entire time of his existence and in all that he undertakes, man walks along all the modal routes together. We can call them "horizontal," while yet by themselves they are without an horizon. For the horizon first opens itself above man's mortal head "vertically," so to speak.[17]

Yet, there is a point where the horizontal routes meet with the horizon. For there is one life-modality in particular that speaks of our responsibility in the history of mankind, namely the historical aspect. It is one *aspect* among all the others. It reminds us that, along the guide-lines of

---

17 The relation between "horizon," "horizontal," "vertical," and "horizonless" is discussed at length in *Radix, Time, and Knowing* (1971) (tr).

which we spoke and from the points of view that we find there, it is us, humans, who *give shape to* history rather than undergoing it. Like all the other aspects, it shows itself in everything where man is at work.

For historicism to call the historical an aspect among others is a degradation of the denominator it has privileged to characterize the whole of history. Therefore it has to reject it resolutely. But the historical shows its specific meaning only in relation with all the other modal aspects. Good and evil, historical progress and historical drawback, can only be ascertained from the center towards which all the modalities converge. History as ongoing succession, time as history, can claim no privilege with regard to this center. For the center of time, the center of all human history, or rather of creation, is a concrete point, settled once for all.[18]

In their convergence upon this center the modalities show the true sense of our activity and of our responsibility for the history of mankind. The totality of human history encloses *all* the modalities, *all* the activities, all that exists, and all that will exist on earth. It is—that is—the history of salvation.

Does this mean that human history as such will save mankind? If that were the case, we would have but a salutary historicism. Since we reject all -isms, we have to reject this one as well. History as the succession as such of what happens or of what men make, decides nothing and leads to nothing, no more than does "nature" and its "time." History as succession is the route of human decisions. But "from above," on the "vertical" line, an objective is being proposed for the history of human decisions. That objective is none other than the destination of creation. Will man go after it?

The two guidelines of time meet in this objective proposed to man. Pushed by the creative dynamism along the mysterious time trajectory, creation is moving towards this destination. Does it depend on man whether it will be reached? We must not evade this question by appeal to a superficial dogma. God does not only speak to us in time (if only we knew what that means), but first of all *through* time, where we hear the sound of his powerful creative dynamics and the dead silence each time the enemy pays its "wages" (Romans 6:23).

---

18 | This is the reason why no historical investigation, and even no hermeneutics, will be able to decide in whatever way, about the true meaning of this point of history. Such investigations can never discover it. Quite to the contrary, it is the meaning of such operations that is determined, right from their start, by the original choice of those who carry them out.

11. Fire

Regarding meaning, we can easily talk in some vague manner. All too readily we present it as enclosed and shackled. We are not allowed to do that. The Christian really falls short when he believes that it is suffi-cient to utter exclamations "for the glory of God" or to use general terms, such as that creation calls us toward the God of Scripture, the true origin of all things. God himself precisely *concretizes* His revelation, His timing being as strict as it is dynamic. He guides the meaning of His creation, of responsible mankind, and of the trajectory of time by the reins of his *kai-roi.* He unfolds His scriptural revelation not only "in the course of time" but even more by "the times and seasons" corresponding to the situation of created man, by way of time and at successive periods according to His sovereign choice.

When it comes to the structural possibilities for making theoretical pronouncements about "velocity" or "history," both the scientist and the theologian are in the same boat. As to the structural conditions for them to utter one word about the results of their investigations, there is no dif-ference between them. But once more we meet with the scheme of nature and grace, or nature and supernature. One well-known version of it reads "common grace and particular grace." But in either form it has led to a good deal of misunderstanding about the christian practice in theoretical endeavors. It is the mark of an inner religious motive that has long since made christian thinking swerve. For secretly the idea of the primacy, that is to say the autonomy, of thinking has sneaked into the theologian's overall theoretical activity. This is the heritage from antiquity and the middle ages, strongly boosted by the revolutionary spirit of humanism.

The result has been the search for the ever more christian correction *of what* was being thought, without realizing before all else that the direc-tion of the route taken could only be determined by its starting point. It was forgotten that the starting point could never be an axiom of thought, but the choice of the *heart* for the Truth. The intellectual starting points and the search for methods depend on this choice.

For the "scientific community" this implies an infinitely compli-cated task that yet cannot be separated from the totality of human com-munion. To start with it we have to be willing. It may seem that a clear testimony is a long way off, but it is to be understood that the theological acceptance of the God of Genesis does not mean much more for the faith of "creation" than the philosophical acceptance of the god of Aristotle or of the deists. If there is nothing more to it than that, the dialectical circle is merely complicated with a new difficulty in the quarrel between theology and the other sciences. The latter will respond by searching for their own appropriate methods.

For the Christian who does not want to live his life of science in any other way than his life of every day—that is to say, according to the saying "As the branch cannot bear fruit by itself, unless it abides in the vine, neither can you, unless you abide in me"—there is only one route, starting from a single point of departure. The first consequence on this route is to comprehend that there is no other way to enter into one's scientific endeavors but by the gate of faith. It needs to be understood that even the modalities of "nature," while remaining natural, anticipate faith via the intermediate modalities of human acts, and that it will never be possible to approach them in a so-called neutral way. For the concept of "thought" is but an abstraction from the living act of *thinking*, the concrete meaning of which is guided by actual faith. Such is the structural ordering of things by the sovereign Creator. For man all positive meaning of his life depends upon a positive faith.

We know that this positive faith is a power of the Spirit of the Word by which all things were made. Time runs its course. As long as man believes that he can continue along the horizontal routes, babbling perhaps about a god of the philosophers or of the theologians, science will but net him only lofty techniques and cultural successes. Access to the truth of reality will, however, not be found on these routes. Rather, they will continue to promote a proud pragmatistic dialectic and a nihilistic despair, since they can only tell us of the passing of time.

The horizontal routes of history and of "civilization" cannot flatter or frighten the Christian who has seen the Word, through which everything was made that was made, emerge through the problems, even of creation's genesis and decline. For on the "vertical" route, he has seen the sign of the promise: the open grave. It rules all the modalities and keeps them in their place, in spite of their painful abuse by the man of science.

Contrary to what a secularized theology wants us to believe, this promise does not assure us of temporal success for civilization, or science, nor for the earthly "churches," as if the kingdom of God "would come in a way striking the eyes of men." Rather, this promise has come to cast fire upon the earth. If we are to hope for an acceptance of the christian message because of what it has to offer for the concerns of the world, then this fire must be extinguished. This is what we see happening around us: empty churches conforming in order to "attract the outside world," and the rise of a pragmatistic Christendom. The believers of the culture that was the fruit of the victory of Easter have silenced the witness of the eternal sacrifice and of the glorious Ascension. But it is impossible to extinguish the fire from Heaven. The ultimate choice will again be put before him who has let himself be dragged along on the roads of the world without accounting for the eternal root with its germinating power.

This root does not superpose some metaphysic upon the positive "realities" that are being studied by the sciences. Far from it. But the force of this root imposes an apriori choice upon the most specialized specialists: Will his thinking go in the direction of the mute appearance of so called facts or "phenomena," in which the autonomous subject is already hidden, or will he move towards the clear horizon of the only Truth? If this horizon does not show itself in the "horizontal" perspective of time, that should in no way discourage him, for in this perspective there is no horizon, nor a promise of success. The horizon of number and of space, of physical movement and of life and history, of knowing and feeling, of faith and of love, and of all that responsible man does and of all that he examines, the horizon of this frightening time with its *kairoi* of trials beyond measure and its probing invitations, the horizon of this disturbing trajectory, investigated in vain by the wisdom of the world—it is death swallowed up in the new creation of God.

TIME FOR REFLECTION

1. Introduction

It is time for Reformational Philosophy to pause for a while to take stock of its situation. Since the thirties of the twentieth century, it has progressed and developed. We now need to ask what has happened to it during this development.

We might be inclined, as is fashionable today, to pose and answer this question by first considering what-all has taken place and then proceed to make comparisons on various points. But what would be the criterion by which such comparisons are made, and what would be the standard for judgment in these matters? Given Reformational Philosophy's warranted pretensions, for it to stoop to a method of compare and contrast is simply out of the question.

Can pretensions ever be warranted? The pretensions of this world are by definition invalid. This means that by raising questions about the development of Reformational Philosophy, we immediately find ourselves at an intersection where the decisive antithesis is to be consciously put in the foreground. For worldly pretensions play a role in our thinking as well, and excluding them starts here. But what exactly is it, then, that we have to exclude? And what kind of question is this?

Can these questions be considered without transcending the boundaries of "pure" philosophy? An affirmative answer to this question would be a response "near to the heart" of the world and supported by its pretensions. So, that decides that.

Yet we have to make ourselves understood even for those whose pretensions we are to reject. Therefore, we will have to explain our negative response in a philosophical fashion. But are we, in trying to do so, not setting ourselves up for what is, on principle, an impossible task?

2. Simple philosophy, useful systematics

Sometimes we hear the suggestion that we should speak in "plain" language. Sometimes it is even asserted that all we have to do is "simply"

This essay was first published in Dutch under separate title in 1973 as *Tijd der Bezinning* (Amsterdam: Buijten en Schipperheijn).

repeat the words of Revelation. Such advice, however, reveals a double misunderstanding. For in the first place, it is supposed that along such "simple" paths we can avoid failure. Secondly, we meet here the identification of Revelation and theo-*logy*: it is supposed that it is possible for the latter to be popularized, simple and free from philosophical complexity.

By way of contrast with this call for simplicity, the "Philosophy of the Cosmonomic Idea" has been applauded for its *philosophical* depth and critical acumen by people who would not refer to themselves as "Christians." This praise for one or another facet of this philosophy was, however, always accompanied by either a rejection of or a silence about its deepest principles. In the meantime, however, also in these quarters, people with less of an eye for its depth and acumen complained, whether sincerely or not, about its "difficulty." Therefore, we need to attend to this assessment with deliberation.

At first, the complaint about difficulty did not come from "philosophical" quarters. In philosophy, people were used to the equally difficult demands from neo-Kantianism and phenomenology. Indeed, this complaint actually arose from "Christian" students who were used to applying the theological recipes that fit with their pretheoretical confessional stock of ideas.

Today, influenced by the pragmatisitic methodologism that arose from the reaction against scholasticism, this procedure of applying theologically informed pat answers is again becoming attractive for the hungry Western mind to feed on.

And this need not surprise us insofar as such thinking does not feel the need to justify itself *as* thinking, but by simply referring to its substratum, to which it is *directed* anyway. Such thinking is then re-assured of its safety by theology, operating as always from the fundamental motive of nature and supernature, even though its two poles are reversed. As in the days of old, it needs to do so out of its own desire for power.

The complaint about difficulty was thus fed from two sides. And it is understandable why both ecclesiastical and non-ecclesiastical "Christians" would have little interest in being bothered by a philosophy that, first of all, asks for an *integral* account of the competence of human thinking and of its structural place. Human thinking did not choose its place; rather, it was *assigned* to it. As a result, it does not have to deal only with its substratum, but above all also with a compelling and propelling superstratum.

There is, therefore, much that needs to be clarified, but it may be understood that the "simplicity" of the complainer is put forward with a lack of awareness of the real threats that come from many sides. It may also be understood that there is also but one remedy, namely insight. Otherwise, it is quite possible that the anesthesia of simplicity will decisively remove all perspective.

Then, from a completely different side, it is claimed that the time has passed for fundamental criticism and that it is urgently needed for reformational philosophy to concentrate on "feeding" the special sciences. Competent adherents should deal seriously with the problems of the special sciences, in order to deal with opposition within these fields.

This demand should not be dismissed. But we have to be conscious of two things. In the first place, the deeper we get into the differences in these special fields, the more the fundamental differences will become relevant. And secondly, something that seems to be especially significant at the moment: reformational philosophy itself is far from consolidated when it comes to its own *philosophical* basics. This lack of consolidation, then, will become acute when engaging the special sciences. Therefore, continued "strategic" reflection continues to be the number one priority. A battle is decided at its fronts, but these fronts require supply *and* central directives.

From the beginning it has been plain that "reformational philosophy," or even the "Philosophy of the Cosmonomic Idea," does not deliver "systematics," even though its thinking is intentionally system*atic* in its structure, due to its theoretical nature. From this systematic tendency the special sciences will benefit, while, on the other hand, a consolidation of its system*atics* will hamper progress. Formulated in the words of this philosophy itself, such consolidation of systematics would foster paralysis in the foundational, retrocipatory, direction of time. What is needed, however, is disclosure.

3. Basic encounter

There appears to be a peculiar directness in the *encounter* with our philosophy. It does not just meet kindred spirits, whether they are scholarly or otherwise; nor does it just meet educated people, who may or may not be adherents. After four decades it is important to notice that our philosophy has become a point of reference beyond such confines. So, what does this philosophy amount to? What is the meaning of its peculiar "directness"?

In order to understand this question, we have to appreciate something about the way the phenomenon "philosophy" has played its part in the *concrete history* of mankind. Today it is being understood as a "discipline." But that is merely to draw attention to a peculiar division of labor. Today this person's attention is here; tomorrow someone else's attention is there. One person studies this discipline, another person studies that discipline. Alternatively, one can look at philosophy as a compartment of the supposed wider field of theory. However, neither in the East nor in the West is this what philosophy was originally all about. Quite to the contrary, it was famous for speaking the ultimate words of wisdom. That is not to say that it was the end of all deliberation. Indeed, it led to the most violent encounters and to the most dynamic developments. Yet the issue was always to clear a path through history for *the* word of wisdom, for truth. That is to say, at stake was the word of central and radical thinking, directed at delimiting and emitting *the* truth itself.

This is what philosophy was, and this is what it has continued to be, right up until the present time, even though it is now clearing its path hidden among the special sciences and life's practice. It has become "suppressed" (*verschwiegene*) philosophy. But still, in its supposition that only methodical-analytical sharpness can bring us in touch with "reality," its concern is with the "truth" about reality. Ever since the time of Parmenides, this was what philosophy was about. All the while, the East steered its own course, right up until recently when the fruits of Western thinking also appeared there to be of benefit for the substratum of life.

So, if philosophy is a matter of fundamental questions and of fundamental encounter, then what do they actually mean who say that christian philosophy should do little more than "echo" Revelation, preferably in as simple a way as possible? Have they explored what actually happens in a philosophical encounter before they start to speak about what christian philosophy should do? Like everybody else, they too go their way in the practice of life and work. They too learn from and make use of the indispensable contributions of the special sciences. Therefore, they are not able to "simply" change the course of history any more than anyone else. Have they asked themselves what is stirring the depths in the fields of their disciplines? Or are they of the opinion that it is sufficient to proceed in a "positive" way?

Such an uncritical attitude may be understandable for the natural scientist. The "positive method" originates indeed from the field of the natural sciences, although even there it should not have the last word. But how about economics, law, linguistics, history, just to mention a few other disciplines? No one engaged in those fields would want to be a "positivist" in the philosophical sense. But some seem to have lost their way there. They are not clear about the basis of their disciplines. Why?

A provisional answer seems obvious. While they had all the time been *nurtured* by the hidden driving motive of "nature and grace" (nature-supernature), they have as well-meaning Christians silently accepted another philosophy. For according to the nature-grace motive, natural reason, though fallible, is sufficient for everyday experience. What exceeds everyday life can only have a meaning that transcends natural reason—though fortunately we are supported by "positive" commands that manage to penetrate our lives here below.

Then there are those we have already mentioned, for whom philosophy can only be effective if it contributes to the debates within the special sciences. They are equally in danger of losing their way. The advocates of "simplicity" forget that philosophy and what they mean by revelation cannot pertain to the same level. As a result, they end up with a popularized "theology" as their standard. The scientific consumers of philosophy, on the other hand, are in danger of losing sight of the *perspective* of philosophy's final questions. *Final* questions, rather than principles. Principles would need no perspective. But the philosophical perspective *receives* its direction *from* guiding principles.

More than ever, this is what is at stake in the philosophical encounter. The scientific parole "forward without looking back" would drive us into the opponents' camp. This is plain from what we observe there. For example, in the field of sociology there is an on-going debate about an analytical vs. a dialectical theory of science such that—bottom-line—the one party is looked at by the other either as a scientific dope or as a social dud. Such mutual exclusion of each other necessarily originates from the rejection of a fundamental perspective as we would understand it. According to the rules of the encounter, any such perspective would entail the judgment of their basic (if even impossible) lie.

4. Historically concrete philosophizing

When we are in need of understanding ourselves, we have to look at the concreteness of our history, both in terms of what we have left behind and of what is still underway. We do not have to be reminded once again of the swift capitulation after the Reformation, when the movement beat a hasty retreat to scholasticism. Nor do we have to evaluate the "kuyperial"[1] era again. What is relevant here is that reformational philosophy arose against the background of two actual historical interests at the time. One was the necessity of a theoretically articulated contribu-

---

1   Mekkes wrote "kuypers," with quotation marks, instead of the regular: Kuyperiaans. I suppose that there is a pun intended here.

tion to the various fields of science. The other was the necessity of finding the central point of the antithesis between christian and nonchristian theoretical worldviews. If the encounter with nonchristian thinking was to be sought in terms of theory, it seemed clear that it would have to be a philosophical encounter. Given the internal structure of theory, there could be no disagreement about this. The only question would be about this pre-condition: that it be an encounter "in terms of theory." Was that really a sufficient condition?

On account of the scholastic tradition in protestant christian circles, this question took the form of a dilemma: transcendent or transcendental criticism? The first of these two would not result in an encounter. It could only lead to a dead end in the exchange. The advocates of "simplicity," who we just discussed, were not ready, or possibly not even willing, to consider the far-reaching consequences of the decision that had to be made on this point, much to the disadvantage of their own scientific endeavors. (On the other hand, it should not be forgotten that a transcendental criticism will ultimately have to justify itself in the courtroom of one's own conscience; that is, it will have to undergo a transcendent critique.)

So, difficulties were bound to arise on this point. From which side, with the aid of which means, and with an emphasis on which points, would the field for the resulting encounter between scriptural and un-scriptural thinking be delineated? Naturally, the answers to these questions were conditioned by the historical circumstances in which they arose. Neo-Kantianism was on the decline, while phenomenology was on the rise. As critical inquiry sharpened, more and more attention was paid to Descartes' ancient certainty "cogito ergo sum," as if it was the only unmoved center in the midst of all the turmoil. In fact, it was the same certainty to which Parmenides had also pointed long ago. While for Descartes and neo-Kantianism it had remained veiled in metaphysics, Husserl rejected Parmenides and Descartes for their several identifications of actual (present) *thinking* with *being*. Yet, in the end, the critical reflection upon the *actual* "cogito"[2] vindicated the thesis of reformational philosophy that Western philosophy had never stopped to regard it as its *archimedean* point. The entire field of theory, with its Gegenstände, had found its delineation around this point, while in this point itself the supposedly irreproachable autonomy of the humanistic man of reason

---

2 The "actual cogito," or "present thinking," is Mekkes's term for supposedly autonomous reason. "Reason" is supposed to be "actual" or "present" in the sense that it is independent of the historical past. See J.P.A. Mekkes, *Radix, Tijd en Kennen* (Amsterdam 1971), p. 22, 25, 35 and § 17 of this text (tr).

appeared to be anchored. What was to be the christian alternative? Such was the common way of formulating the problem. But the question may be asked: How was the problem taken materially?

In the search for an alternative, the humanistic thesis was in fact accepted as the point to start from. But, again, the question may be asked: should the intended alternative have a parallel structure? Evidently, the possibility of such a formal parallelism was assumed—apparent in the continued use of the expression "archimedean point." The difference was supposed to be a matter of content, while the way in which humanism defined that content—as the terms of the traditionally so-called "Gegenstand relation"—was regarded to be matter of the structure of theoretical thinking as sovereign in its own sphere. This brings us again to probably the most poignant questions in relation to the call for reformational philosophy to go "forward" into the special sciences. Was this the path to follow? Or should reformational philosophy have called for continued control, also from the side of the sciences, of its deepest foundations given philosophy's nature as an activity at the *boundaries* of thought?

5.   Philosophy and groundmotive

Outside the circles from which reformational philosophy took root, it was commonly accepted that philosophy is an activity at the frontiers of thought. For it was well understood that philosophical criticism can time and again stir the special sciences to significant development. As we saw, this was the reason that reformational philosophy was initially met with more or less indirect interest. The sharp critical development of humanistic philosophy strongly stimulated reflection regarding the boundaries of thought (even though this reflective activity was, as before, aimed at saving *thinking* itself). A prime example is the pointed discussions within the Frankfurt school of thought. But within Reformed circles in the Netherlands, philosophical criticism had been practically unknown, except for a few professional philosophers.

The brute forces of horizontalism[3] have actually exposed a lack of orientation in Reformed circles. What is the reason for this lack? If it is due in part to internal theoretical factors, the serious question that arises for reformational philosophy is whether it can rest on its laurels and simply continue to pay attention to internal theoretical problems without engaging in a *continuous* critical check of its own foundations and what follows from them.

---

3   By "horizontalism" Mekkes means horizontalistic theology. He considers it to be the common enemy of both reformational philosophy and "verticalism" (tr).

Those who adopt the horizontalist approach have known from the get-go that compromise with regard to the fundamentals of reformational philosophy is out of the question; hence their tried and tested tactic of negation. And so, where the "Kuyperian" standard is no longer carried with conviction, many descendants, from *those* quarters who were already intuitively predisposed against foundational reformational reflection anyway if not also numbed by the "culturism" of the lower middle class, will instinctively oppose reformational philosophy. Where in the boundary area are we to look for the spiritual, structural causes of this opposition that are of vital interest to reformational philosophy?

The kind of root we are looking for cannot be found in the area of theory. Theory is merely a *partial* area. The kind of root we are looking for has to be integral in its nature and origin. That is to say, there is a deepest *ground*motive at work in producing and driving such a root. A groundmotive governs life in its entirety; it is a driving motivation of root and origin. The particular groundmotive that is at work here is the groundmotive of nature and grace (supernature).

It is well known. There is no need to describe it again. But what did it *do*? What was its *effect* in the history of this recent period, and what, consequently, is its effect upon us nowadays? It withdrew from "grace," which was dubbed "special," and concentrated on "nature," which was dubbed "common grace." On the "above" side there was something eternal at stake; fortunately there was support from "below" in the guise of scientific theological insights. While the "below" itself was bound to an ethical and intellectual assignment where "natural reason," enlightened as usual by theology, could lay out the cards.

This resulted in the dichotomy between the sphere of "supernature," where the activities were regulated by ecclesiastical guidance, and the sphere of "nature," where the activities were to be aimed at showing creation its temporal destination along the tracks laid out from above. There was a temporal "creation" and an eternal "hereafter." They both belonged to God, and to both of them the believer was supposed to contribute. But, having left traditional Thomism behind, where would we find the formula to distinguish between these two spheres? The attempts at "common grace" solutions are well known. But with regard to these schemes, just as with the medieval and older schemes, we have to ask for the justification for such a dichotomy. Instead, it had been simply pronounced by the "thinking of being." So there, behind theology, science, and practice, was philosophy, alive and kicking as it had been all along—theoretical in its origin and method, but having its say in central decisions of universal significance. How could it acquire such influence, and what was to be expected from that for the future? What was its perennial influence in the pulpit or in the laboratory or among those who sought political power by appealing to the prejudices, emotions, fears, and expectations of the public? Why is it that philosophy befuddles more "simple-minded" folks to the point that they want nothing to do with it any more? And what is its power such that it makes "intellectuals" believe in the exclusive significance of the formulas they construct about reality?

Assigning philosophy a place within one of the sectors of the full gamut of life is both possible and legitimate. But we should never forget that others will fiercely object to any such assignment, and most decidedly so by ignoring it. Alternatively, it is possible to suggest that theology or the sciences should supersede philosophy. However, it will only re-emerge in the midst of the competition itself. If I attempt to control it rationally, it has always been there first. Neither by "simplicity" nor by the most elaborate theoretical construction can I get rid of its conceptual priority. In short: its boundary-character subjects Western intellectuals to the most thorny demands, namely, of having to make boundary-distinctions. And that means that truthful philosophizing can never rest in "consolidation," not even if it be merely provisional.

In the meantime, "horizontalism" forces thinking to explore this tricky boundary area, which was discerned by Nietzsche and which got the better of Heidegger. Precisely because of its boundary character, both adherents and opponents within reformed circles have made a choice with regard to reformational philosophy. Christians outside reformed circles made this choice in a vague sort of way because they either felt that they could not ignore its critical appeal, or because they felt that they could not overlook its christian appeal. These were exceptions, however.

6. Boundary area

A boundary area is not itself the boundary. And the crucial question is this: Can the boundary be crossed? This critical question can only be answered *after* crossing *through* this side of the boundary area. If philosophy is the boundary area in this simile, then the question is: What is on the other side of philosophy? What is beyond the boundary? There is no way the intellectual can rely upon mere intellectual in-sight in order to answer this question. He is coming from "this" side. Or would there be another option for him? Could he attain to some quasi-insight maybe, one that would come close to some kind of over-sight?

Neither Nietzsche nor Heidegger tried to conceal the embarrassment brought on them by this question and each in his own way, and exclusively with an eye to safeguard "this side," gave an answer. But in no way could their answer reach beyond the boundary area. All it could do was to repeat the dogmatic hypothesis concerning the nature of the boundary, namely the fundamental dialectics of humanism: autonomy versus rational compulsion. This is the ultimate border for humanism. It is a limit that cannot be transgressed.

Today's "horizontalism" has left existentialism behind and now wallows in methodological positivism. In league with the humanism of our day, it has autonomously cast its lot with the counter-pole of personal autonomy, namely, rational control. It had no choice, since it had itself sprung from the groundmotive of nature-and-supernature and had to hold on to that groundmotive because "theology" appeared to depart from the field outside of its domain. Theology could only be effective within the boundary area insofar as it was originally designed to assist in the approach of the boundary itself by means of rational faith distinctions. In other words, if theology wants to retain its competence in speaking about the boundary, it must limit its activity to the boundary area between here and beyond. This is the area where Western wisdom from of old keeps the first and the last word to itself. Therefore, the theologian will have to make a choice here: either he maintains his parity with the inhabitants of the boundary-area, or he takes orders from *yonder* side. But the latter would mean abdicating the primacy of the Western intellect, which, backed by the entire tradition of his trade, he must avoid at all costs. Therefore, in order to keep his footing, he has to adapt his dealing about the "supernatural" to what is nowadays in control on the "natural" side, namely, pragmatic positivism.

In former days priority had usually been ascribed to supernature. This was in line with the shape of society in those days. Nowadays, the church and theology do not get a hearing if they are not ready to capitulate to the "nature" motive in its modern guise—the guise of modern methodologism, which, after the manner of the natural sciences, expresses "truth" in formulae so as to enhance its practical effect. Thus, we see supernatural theology today taking its place within the boundary area *under* the reign of the method of "nature"; no longer much interested in the "yonder side," but with religious fervor directing all its interest to the transitory *substratum* of life. Hardly anyone wants to recognize this. There is no inkling that the boundary area—philosophical thinking— might constitute a treacherous domain. And it seems impossible to discern the terror of the reign of darkness in the enemy's ethical masquerade.

Naturally, horizontalism is not the result of theoretical delibera-tion—however much it avails itself of it. It is merely a temporal guise of the power of apostasy, whose opportunity has come due to theoreti-cal and practical scholasticism's confusing demolition over the centuries along and near the boundary—a demolition that has touched the hearts of men, and that extends from there into thought and practice. These ruins tell us much about the zone where today a scriptural philosophy has to set to work. It knows that it is not able to find the boundary by itself, let alone prepare the path to traverse it. But it does have the crea-turely theoretical task to trace out the map of this area. And not only that. It also has the task of putting up warning signs at those places and junctions where choices have to be made. The intellectual enemy is not so much the problem as is the spiritual enemy behind it. Is this enemy being discerned?

Let us, for the moment, leave behind the "horizontalist" opponent. Let us pay attention to a question coming from another, equally impor-tant, side, but a question that penetrates far more deeply: Why should we pay attention to the "boundary area" when it is the boundary itself that is decisive, and while we have only one distinction to make, namely: this side or the other one, here or beyond?

This is a theological question and intentionally posed over against "horizontalism." But if it presupposes a theology of the supernatural, we must again first pay attention to a prior philosophical question regarding the boundary area, namely: What is the relationship between the poles of nature and supernature? And further: What is the origin of the tension implied in this distinction? Is it a legitimate distinction? These questions will probably lead to a definitive search for the route, while the common enemy of horizontalism is kept at bay.

7. Antithesis

Recently, dialectical theology has given voice to some penetrating supernatural declarations. And it is worth noting that this was real "theo-logos," just like the old scholastic theology. While old scholasticism was formed, within the nature-supernature scheme, by joining with the ra-tionalistic wisdom of ancient Greek philosophy, dialectical theology took its shape from the basic driving motive of the philosophy of existence. Old scholasticism darkened the Light of Scripture in the boundary zone by mixing it with Aristotle's theory of forms. Dialectical theology did the same by mixing it with Karl Jaspers' (and others') ideas of existence and transcendence. In both cases, the theological mixing was orchestrated by

41

human reason. In the latter case it was human reason in conjunction with the existentialistic idea of autonomy.

The nature-supernature motive was itself already dialectical in nature. So was the humanistic groundmotive with which it joined forces, even in the guise it derived from Kierkegaard-Jaspers-Heidegger. That is why "nature" was left open for every possible influence upon human life from the opposite pole of humanism. And so, ultimately, a methodological materialism took over.

Theoretical interest in the philosophy of existence and the humanistic idea of autonomy was confined to some philosophical and theological specialists. Meanwhile, everyday life as well as most of the sciences willingly submitted to the dictates of materialistic methodology.

Horizontalism fervently used the twilight in the border zone for materialistic purposes. But it is not surprising that from another side an appeal is made to the idea of *freedom* and that there is even a reference in this appeal to the harmful influence of dialectical theology within this development towards horizontalism. This should make us sensitive to a difficult question.

We do not hesitate to declare that in the struggle against demonic horizontalism we are closely allied to a movement that in square opposition draws attention to the root-antithesis between the Rule of God and what the Gospel calls "this world." So far, we used the terms "border" and "border zone" mainly to indicate the philosophical questions that urge themselves upon us here. By "border" we mean the boundary that delineates God's revelation of Himself on the one side and man's receiving of that revelation on the other side. The question we have to ask at this point is: does this "border" coincide with the line of antithesis we have just mentioned?

Naturally we do not want to deny God the supremacy over this (our) side of the "border." Neither did Luther mean to do this in his controversial idea of the two kingdoms ("*Ich bin von Ockham's Schule*"). But for us the border is the one between *giving* Revelation on the one hand and seeking-to-*receive* it on the other hand. In this seeking-to-receive, the history of Christendom evidences a mixing and confusing of confidence in Scripture with confidence in human wisdom. This was a systematic and, in many respects, an organized confidence. This is why, given the rise of horizontalism, attending to the "border zone" is so critically important. For ages it has been under the control of the *basic*—beyond critical questioning—driving motive of nature-and-supernature. And no matter how well-intended, this deliberated confidence was in fact nothing but an

attempt to wipe the border out. It was in truth an attempt against Revelation, and as such an attempt mounted against "yonder side." The rise of
horizontalism is proof of the fact that a choice must be made to counter
any such attempt. In the border zone men fight a bitter struggle between
age-old parties, one after the other of which claims the right to identify
the border check-point with its own position. The means are always new,
but the driving motive is always the same.

For him who would be guided solely by God's Spirit and who, *in*
faith, is at the same time permanently engaged in drawing reasoned distinctions, this is confusing. How is he to keep his bearing and remain ori-
entated towards the border? Should we not counter horizontalism with
a radical "verticalism"? Do not the biblical words "forgetting what lies
behind" (Philippians 3:13) mean that we should ultimately forget about
what lies on this side of the border? But would that not imply that "this
side" thereby becomes an area that does not matter?

The answer to such questions cannot but come from the "other
side," the only side that is competent in these matters. But have we not
already received an answer? Why did He, from Whom alone we can receive what we need, descend *below* all border zones and *below* all areas
on this side? What was His "business" here? Was it "only" to take away a
confusing mist and leave a traveler's guide behind? We are now approaching a very central spot in the border zone. Here lies a decisive question for
a battle-ready philosophy.

8. Vantage point?

To continue our discussion, rich in the terminology of confrontation: Where can we find a point from which to survey the battle?[4] To raise
the question is to answer it, for every supposed vantage point itself will be
fought over; that has been so from the beginning of human history, and
will remain so till its end.

One could try to occupy such a point, either by reasoning or by
a speculative leap. But, in either case, one is immediately tossed about
between the poles of nature and supernature, and subsequently between
the poles of the "nature"-motive one assimilates (either of antiquity or
of humanism). There is no escape from battle in the border zone. Long
ago, the *radical* adversary drew back from boundary questions since he
does not recognize any legitimate boundary standing in the way of his
sovereignty. When all is said and done he can only look with pity at what

---

4   Cf. Herman Dooyeweerd's reference to a "tower" above the landscape in *A
New Critique of Theoretical Thought* I, 8.

he sees as inherently contradictory endeavors. He may even possibly have some sympathy for the philosophical effort thus expended.

What has a "philosophy of science" under his régime got to do with boundaries? For the adversary, "border zone" can only mean one thing: there are frontiers that science has yet to conquer. Where, for the moment, progress has proven to be *too* difficult, the prevailing wisdom will adopt a "dialectical" method: conceding that there may even be an ultimate horizon—"the reality of universals"—even though it is hardly permissible to call them by that name. For those humanistic travelers in the border zone, who still care about possible threats to human autonomy, the border remains an uncertain and fluctuating line between the horizons of theory and of time.[5]

For centuries philosophy has been full of confidence in raising its pretentious voice. But even though today it has to consider whether it is still wise to mention itself by name, its real character becomes ever more apparent, whether it be blatantly manifest or silently hidden away in the special sciences: its pesudo-*revelational* character causes confusion in the border zone. *That* is why the motive of nature-and-supernature is the most treacherous of all apostate motives.

The real border is the border of outright sovereign revelation, which is impervious to human thought. But under the sway of the nature-supernature motive the search for *real* Revelation was from the start perverted into a search for pseudo-Revelation. So then: what point is there in looking for a vantage point from which to assess one's overall position, and thereby survey one's battle prospects prior to making a forward thrust toward the border? After all, a thinker in this confusing position is all the while fully engaged on this side, ordering his own affairs while in combat with his contemporary philosophical opponents.

The nature-supernature motive is simply misleading. It hides the fact that every human search for such a strategic point from which to plot an advance against the border is futile. Yet, man has time and again attempted to locate such a point, convinced that he will only be able to attain ultimate knowledge by his own thinking. At first this conviction was silently adopted, but since the beginning of "modernity" this conviction has become a very conscious one: it has to be theoretical thinking, bequeathed by history, that will yield this pinnacle of knowledge. While still dominated by old scholasticism, it was theology, as the special philosophy of the supernatural, that attempted to produce such knowledge. It subjected Scripture to (believing) reason, but also assumed itself capable

---

5   See my *Radix, Tijd en Kennen.*

of determining the point from which the revelational lines of Scripture can be drawn and from which the relation between Scripture and human wisdom in the "border zone" of creation can be surveyed.

Ever since horizontalism, in the name of reason and "charity," subsumed the sphere of supernature *under the category of* "*nature*," it has consistently relegated every account of a groundmotive to the rank of philosophical myth. Yet, in doing so, it has made us aware that without the critical question that we raise here, our theoretical thinking, in attempting to reach beyond its own competence, will be doomed to fruitless fatigue without end, just as our practical pursuits will be doomed to wandering aimlessly among our own delusions.

After centuries of grappling in vain, the time has come to leave all faith in pseudo-revelation behind once and for all and to jettison the confusions in the border zone wrought by horizontalism. If we then meet a fellow combatant in the border zone who is nevertheless expecting an immediate answer that transcends revelation from yonder side, this can only encourage us even more to gain insight, even if we are to go on without a vantage point. But where shall this insight be found?

9. Choice of direction

The so-called "Philosophy of the Cosmonomic Idea" is operating in the border zone alongside other philosophies—worldly pseudo-revelations, some hidden among the special sciences, others openly displayed. It goes about its business, well aware that it is *not* itself a "revelation." Yet, both to its adherents as to its opponents, it sometimes appears as such. Opponents presume it to carry the pretension of revelation because they cannot tolerate any revelation beyond their own wisdom. Therefore, they assume that the Philosophy of the Cosmonomic Idea has absorbed some (obviously unacceptable) revelatory elements, but never that it could really be driven by a sovereign revelation. Consequently, they dismiss the deep level of its "transcendental criticism" as an ingenious though nevertheless shallow, logical argument—the expression of a dogmatic *apriori*. Adherents, on the other hand, have too often equated it with some reformational school or denomination. They failed to realize that it is a theoretical attempt by structurally appropriate means to counter the revelatory pretensions of the worldly philosophies. Transcendental criticism aims at showing that, after all, there is nothing more than *mere theory* in such pseudo-revelation.

However, if Reformational philosophy is convinced that it is driven by the living *groundmotive* of Scripture—which is none other than creation's groundmotive—to counter pseudo-revelation at the theoretical level in order "to bear testimony before them," then it must always intentionally work to keep itself wholeheartedly under the influence of this groundmotive. It was conceived and raised in the midst of philosophy and theology. Therefore, it will first of all have to continue to unravel the confusion in the "border zone." On the one hand it has to realize that this confusion is endemic to its heritage, and on the other hand that any remaining confusion will sooner or later avenge itself in the mêlée in the special sciences and in practice. That is why its transcendental criticism, as well as the elaboration of its structural principles, may in no way ever be considered complete or nearly complete. Ongoing reflection, more intensive than that of any other philosophy, must be the order of the day. And it must be structural reflection. "Simplification" serves no end, and systematization with an eye to scientific "utility" will only frustrate the effort to strengthen the worldview and the battlefront in the sciences. In practice this means that those who labor in these areas will continually have to contribute to this dynamic philosophical reflection.

When it comes to the relationship between the *integral Revelation* of Truth and its engagement of theoretical philosophy (as well as every other sector of life), the so-called "groundmotive" is crucial. This term seeks to indicate clearly that the reformational believer professes creation as it is given to be the revelation of a persisting power. As regards nature, this power reveals itself as an upholding power in the midst of all changes. As for humankind, it reveals itself in our calling to engage in continuous *disclosure*.

"Disclosure" does not mean to suggest that creation and its relationship to humankind could be significant *in and of itself.* Here lies one of the most serious confusions in the border zone, mainly due to the motive of nature-supernature. Strictly speaking, it makes no sense to speak of unchangeable "states-of-affairs." Therefore, what some "orthodox" Christians refer to as the "cultural mandate" can never have any meaning in itself. Man's ultimate calling to be "God's co-worker" binds the human community to its basic constituency in creation. But creation's dynamic "movement" is part and parcel of this constituent "state." Therefore, humans are called to *direct* creation's movement, to direct it in a particular direction, namely, towards the *border.*

Here, in the border zone, we have to listen philosophically—which is not to say that "philosophy" is the ultimate listener. Rather, it is the *philosopher* who is eminently equipped to listen. The question is: What will be the direction of the philosophical reflection that *results from* his listening? And what will be the direction of the practice in theory and life that, consciously or not, makes use of the philosopher's "services"?

It is far from certain that it will be the right direction. Quite the contrary! By virtue of creation's movement along the track of time, man continually has to choose direction *towards* his Origin, *towards* humankind's Creator. But he continues, time and again, to choose the wrong direction. That we know this is not the result of philosophical inquiry in the border zone. The philosophical pursuit of understanding here not only comes up empty; the very attempt deceitfully leads us astray. For we can know, via another route, that we cannot understand this by mere thinking. Thoughtful living and live thinking must have another starting point. Our natural inclination is to deny this, for otherwise our autonomy and any "reasonable" foundation for such autonomy would be destroyed. That is why Nietzsche and Heidegger both refused to draw the obvious conclusion from their philosophizing and why modern methodologism has radically turned on its heels. That is also why theologism hates the Book, and why it has turned it into its "object."

As a result of all this, reformational philosophy in the course of its development had to face two closely-related questions. If it was to give direction to the philosophical discussion on the basis of its own starting point it had to answer them both. The first was: What precisely is the significance and the content of this so-called "starting point"? As we saw, this question arose when the possibility of engaging other philosophies in authentic discussion on a philosophical level had to be considered. The subsequent question became: What is the direction we have to take from this "starting point"? This question complicated the former. It arose when in the search for a possible point of contact we hit upon the basic motives that on either side drive philosophical development but that can neither be reduced to anything deeper, nor to one another. And while the groundmotives of antiquity, scholasticism, and humanism appeared to be historically and decisively one in their presumption of the autonomy of human reason, reformational philosophy radically rejected this premise. How, then, could there be a starting point for mutual discussion?

10. Archimedean Point?

As we saw in paragraph 4, given the historical circumstances, it seemed possible that the actual "cogito" of the theoretical "Gegenstand relation" of the (neo-)Kantian schools could serve as such a starting point for the discussion. For the issue was: can the certainty of our knowing be based in theoretical thinking? Theory of knowledge had become the prime concern of the philosophical prolegomena. It was assumed to be the only possible starting point for certain knowledge. According to the Kantian tradition, the act of knowing occurred between on the one hand the moment to moment actuality of the "I think" (in abstraction from the content of "I") and the chosen "field of investigation" on the other.

Hegel had pointed out that requiring a theory of knowledge to precede the process of knowing seems very much like wanting to learn to swim without venturing into the water. He had also observed that the "object" being "for it" (for the subject) derives its meaning from the togetherness of subject and object "for us." According to him, the meaning of the object could only be fulfilled in a continuing process of reflection by the "spirit" in its aspiring to "absolute" self-knowledge. Although Husserl began with the Kantian configuration, he gradually became convinced of Hegel's more profound insight. But in *Radix, Time, and Knowing* I argued that Husserl in fact did not dispense with the idea of the "actual" cogito.

At first the Philosophy of the Cosmonomic Idea took the opposition of actual thinking and "Gegenstand" to be a responsible starting point for the epistemological comparison between itself and neo-Kantianism, supposing that this was the first thing necessary.

The only reservation expressed at this point, somewhat in analogy with Hegel, but without referring to him, was that the Gegenstand relation was itself an *abstract* configuration. Yet, within theoretical thinking, and certainly within epistemology, it was considered to have its own rightful place. (The principle of sphere-sovereignty, of the distinctive integrity of theoretical thought or "science" within its own sphere, may have played a role here.)

The Philosophy of the Cosmonomic Idea referred to all philosophy that considered generally valid knowing to be based in theory as "immanence" philosophy. It countered immanence philosophy with a "transcendental criticism," by pointing out that the "cogito" (I think), as such, is itself merely one function among all that is real. Therefore, it could by itself never accomplish the synthesis between itself and the content of its field of investigation. All attempts at such a synthesis would of necessity go astray, torn between various modal denominators, giving rise to confusing antinomies. The entire history of theoretical pursuit gives evidence of this. All attempts to "talk through" such confusions automatically slip from one antinomy to another. Only a philosophy that turns from the immanence standpoint to a stance in the root of the reality-to-be-distinguished can clear the way for a united search for knowledge of the various facets and sectors of reality and their interrelations. The question now is:

What is this root? This is a serious question, since it has appeared from our argumentation that it can not be designated by "thinking," or any other function, for that matter.

Thus, the Philosophy of the Cosmonomic Idea placed another fixed point over against the "I think," the "fixed point" of immanence philosophy, namely the point in which all "functions," thinking included, have their root. And we were invited to first take our common stance there, in order to gain an overview and to choose a method, in short, to actually accomplish the synthesis between thought and its "object."

However, if it is a point beyond all temporal functional coherence, then it cannot be found by thinking about it. In that case, the invitation refers to a sphere beyond the reach of "immanence philosophy." Even more to the point, and this is decisive, the question becomes urgent how man, who lives *in* time, can actually know about this point. How can he find his way towards it? And how can he hold his ground in the battle about it? After all, man finds himself on "this side" of the "border"—where Western pseudo-revelation points exclusively at what can be reached by way of thought. Consequently, the invitation to come together will be met by the reproach that it is an invitation loaded with ambiguity. For how can this "mutual" search for truth be undertaken if it presupposes a stance that, at root, is unavailable to the discussion partner on this side of the border? Indeed, how can it be mutual if the one proposing such a search can only take such a stance by going beyond the common arena? Yet, the question remains: How are we going to reach it? And further, how are we to hold our ground?

For the one party the point beyond all questioning is considered to be the "archimedean" point that is anchored in thought. But the other party realizes that such terminology does not fit his case, simply because there is nothing for man to "anchor." For this insight he can thank Husserl and his student Heidegger. They caught a glimpse of this. At the same time, the cause of their failure, especially that of Heidegger, was an even more alarming beacon for him.

Consequently, the road is changed for reformational philosophizing. Transcendental criticism should direct its attention to the dynamics of the driving forces, the "groundmotives" for acting and thin*king*. On this road, epistemology must give up its traditionally supposed primacy. Warned by the confusions in the border zone, it will carefully take heed lest it engage its "transcendent" critique prematurely. Thus the questions of border, driving force, and structure should be considered with even greater urgency.

11. Motivations

The questions about border, motive, and structure are closely related. Does the motivation originate from beyond the border? Is its origin beyond human reason as such? Or should any dealings with it be rejected if it does not originate from "this" side? The answer to these questions has immediate implications for the question about "structure." The order of all structure, from the simplest material particle to the most far reaching human inspiration, is a dynamic order: all structure springs from and awaits human motivation. For human beings (*must*) take action—action taken here in the widest possible sense, including "acts" and aspirations—which is impossible without the universal "substratum" of human temporal existence: dynamic natural objects.

Hence the question as to the source of human motivation is the ultimate (or first) question that can be asked. And if it cannot be answered by reason, then, if reason holds its own decision about itself to itself, it cannot but perpetuate the confusion in the "border zone." And if reason, with some variant of scholasticism, would take part in a discussion on "this" side about a supposed origin on "yonder" side, it would even add to the confusion.

Every attempt to decide from "here," with or without an appeal to "there," will entangle the thinker in a fundamentally dialectical ground-motive: either that of rational form vs. chaotic matter (antiquity), or that of autonomy vs. intellectual control (humanism), or that of nature vs. supernature (scholasticism). It is the latter that we found to be the most confusing and treacherous. In early and high mediaeval scholasticism, philosophy and the theology of the supernatural joined with the Greek form motive. In the late middle ages the principle of arbitrariness (chaotic matter) penetrated both stories. Nineteenth century theologizing wanted to join with the autonomy principle of humanism in its idealistic and post-idealistic hey-days. And in the twentieth century dialectical theology sought to join forces with existentialism.

In all of these cases, the biblical sovereignty of God—though often tampered with by rationalism or irrationalism—continued to be regarded as having supernatural primacy over "nature." In other words: Within this dialectical *motive,* primacy was attributed to the idea of the supernatural. Today horizontalistic theology has turned this order upside-down. In the groundmotive that drives it, God's spoken and creational Revelation is subsumed under man's temporal existence, which is considered to be integrally accessible to theoretical and practical reason. Consequently, it is thought that Scriptural revelation is to be read exclusively from the side of human existence as understood by reason. Not all of the well-known adherents of horizontalism comply with this anti-norm, but that does not change its inherent absoluteness. What we are dealing with here is motivation that is *basic*, which means that it holds beyond any critical doubt.

Hopefully, these explanations will remove some of the confusion in the border zone, and make the real line of demarcation more visible. It is not possible for man by temporal means of his own choosing to cross the border between the meaning-fullness of Truth on "yonder" side and the reality on this side within which he lives. Consequently, he cannot even know that border. If he knows anything of yonder side, it is only by means determined by and supplied from that side.

This means is Revelation. Revelation is *the* Dynamic Power. It is the power of the Word that called the creature into being. And it is also the force that *spoke to* the creature, in order that it would understand the meaning of its being-there. *Revelation* is the basic driving *motive* of creation. As such it demands to be recognized. How and where can it be known? Where is its point of application for man, the representative and head of creation? How does he get to the starting point of the line of Revelation? We have formulated the groundmotives of the pseudo-revelations of this world. How can we formulate the groundmotive of Scripture? Can it be formulated at all? After all, it is the living and life-giving force itself, beyond all form-giving from our side. It is clear that it cannot evoke a dialectical counter-pole, for it is exclusive in its working and speaking. Can we even presume to indicate it by means of a coherent statement?

Creation, of which we are a part, is a broken creation. But its rupture is not the seeming rupture ascribed to it by various dialectical configurations; rather, it is the radical rupture between two "parties." That is why the "Philosophy of the Cosmonomic Idea" has attempted, over against the groundmotives of this world, to formulate the scriptural-creational motive as "creation-fall-redemption." In this formula the middle term is ultimately undone, while the first term is restored in its full meaning. Why did we choose this order in our formulation?

If it is the power of this groundmotive that sovereignly determines the meaning of the created cosmos, then it can only be understood out of the very same Word that posits and directs the creature from the other side of the border. If reformational philosophy wants to articulate the scriptural groundmotive in the battle against pseudo-revelation, then there is no other way for it, but to follow the word of Scripture. But, given the situation in the border zone, this involves a danger.

As we saw before, the potential danger is that philosophy mixes revelation with pseudo-revelation; something too often encouraged by theology, which ever since the first century has failed to develop a scripturally-critical attitude. Revelation's Book became a textbook, an "object" for reasoned christian thought. The idea was that the faithful reader of Scripture would "believe" and accept as true what is incomprehensible or unacceptable from the standpoint of common sense. His "reason," which was regarded to be the true essence of man, would then be able to understand the Creator's word from Scripture according to the order of rational thought. Consequently, the line of revelation could only be seen to start at the beginning of scriptural history. It would run its course along the lines of the calendar, in order to finally lead to the prophecy of the "end." The explication of this order was supposed to be given in the historical line of revelation itself. Any subsequent "hermeneutics," if it appears to be necessary, would have to be executed along (believing) *scientific* lines. In spite of its rejection of all scholastic or semi-scholastic motivations, reformational philosophy, in its formulation of the groundmotive of Scripture, bound itself to this way of ordering the givens of Scripture.

This brings us back to our current concern with horizontalism. For horizontalism there is no longer any meaning in what scholasticism had come to regard as "belief." The control of "natural" thought by a "supernatural" authority has today been inverted. For the understanding of Revelation this does not get us any further than some explanation of the retrocipatory analogies of faith, while the *meaning* of these analogies can only be rendered by actual belie*ving*. This is also true of horizontalism. But because its faith is directed towards ("anticipates") scientific methodological thinking as such, this remains beyond its grasp.

The meaning of Scripture's "groundmotive" eludes horizontalism. It defines the task of thinking about "supernature" by a materialistic understanding of the Gospel and of redemption. Redemption becomes a matter of man by man in time. The only motives to be recognized are economistic-materialistic ones, evaluated by epicurean standards, possibly guided by some gospel chorus of models derived from methodological thought.

When the scriptural meaning of sovereign creation and the scriptural meaning of redemption disappear, each and every real meaning of the term "fall" disappears. Horizontalism's integrally driving groundmotive is that of humanism, pressing on for an "autonomy" of total, rational control.

Even while reformational philosophy was still hanging on to the after-effects of the supernature-nature motive, Christians both inside and outside its circle could not but have strong reactions to horizontalism. Did it not turn the entire ecclesiastical *status quo* upside down? Responses generated by a consistent verticalism, mentioned earlier, are a case in point. While horizontalism will not hear of a "yonder side," for verticalism the voice and the force from the other side is the only thing that counts. As a result of this, the groundmotive's "creation" was for all practical purposes swallowed by the "fall." The only thing left to expect with respect to creation became its annihilation in "the end."

Horizontalism obtains its one-sided perspective in the midst of the obfuscation that prevails in the border zone. Any "other side" could at most be a "hypothesis" meted out by the grace of "this side." Clearly, but falsely, the archimedean point recognized here is *in* one's own thinking. This adds considerably to the urgency of a question that is decisive for both radical verticalism and reformational philosophy. Because both desire to oppose this apostate horizontalism with force, it is extremely important that they discern their point of departure correctly. In other words, will it be possible to get to a clear view of the "point of application" for the hermeneutics of the history of creation?

It cannot be an "archimedean" point, not a point that is, where "I" can take my stance in order to survey the moving situation. Quite the contrary. It is a point from which all movement and the dynamics of my existence, together with that of all other people, originates. Yet, without knowledge of it, I will never be able to choose my course, let alone keep to it. But then how can I find it? And how am I going to chart any orientation from there? It is from "yonder side" that I have been placed on this side. How then am I going to get any knowledge of such a point from "this" side? How shall I do that, if it is not pointed out to me from the other side? And when I am impressed by what is being shown to me, how then shall I recognize the right perspective, so that I will *understand* the *Truth*, discriminating between it and the lies of "this world"? Reason, as such, cannot instruct me here. But then, equally, a "rational" following of the trajectory of revelation will not show me its point of departure, nor map its path. It will not be possible to formulate the *ground*motive of revelation from "yonder side" along a line of history. For any such line can only be recognized by virtue of the power that comes from that motive itself. And man has no choice but to be seized *by* that Motive—now.

53

12. Sovereign motivation and human history

Originally the revelation of the sovereign Creator is and remains beyond our "grasp." Yet it is truly remarkable that He brings it to us as the history of *our own* existence—about which, as a matter of life and death, we have a vital "interest"—while yet it cannot be understood *from* that history by itself. Revelation can neither be understood from the outside nor from the inside of history. The assumption that it could be understood from outside of history is simply an error due to faith in the rational form-motive of scholasticism. And that the understanding of revelation would be possible through history is the mistaken view of a dialectical or evolutionistic historicism.

Revelation is incompatible with any worldly groundmotive. It does not square with any worldly view of time either. Revelation *eternally* transcends both. Yet, it is noteworthy that the eternality of the *living* God has nothing to do with any "idea" we construe on the basis of our concepts of time.

In order to make His intentions clear to us, God not only speaks to us in our language and in our concepts, nor does he only use specific images and experiences. He speaks to us as we are, in our suffering and rejoicing, in our loving and not-loving, in our struggles, in our choices about what is right and what is wrong. He speaks to us in the experience of our everyday possibilities, as well as in the experience of our limitations, in our successes and in our failures. Above all in the pain that we inflict upon and suffer from each other, personally and in the history of nations and societies and their revolutionary factions. It was from these realities *as such* that the Master took His illustrations and parables. Without a truly live sense of what creation and the history of mankind show every one every day, it would have been impossible to understand what the Giver of revelation had said from of old, to Israel, and in the "fullness of time." What would the recipients of revelation have understood of its all-decisive center if they had not known of the force of death in and around them, and of the impossibility to look beyond it? How could the multitudes have been bound to the Master's words, if in their all-sided daily experience they had not felt the inexplicable gravitational pull of earthly existence? And how, finally, could that which it is all about have exerted its victorious power in the *hearts* of the disciples if they had not been prepared for its reception in a "creaturely" way? If from out of their *earthly* existence they had not been filled with a heartfelt desire to learn this one message: "The hour is coming, and *now is*, when the *dead* will hear the voice of the Son of God, and those who hear will *live*"? (John 5:25).

Who dares to take this living comfort away by somewhere in the background still holding on to the possibly "contradictory" effects of the nature-supernature motive? After all, "supernature," a fancy of earthly thinking, disappears in the mist, leaving mortal man behind in the agony of his temporal existence. But the Son of God appeared *here*, and it is *here* that he desires to rule over men. And *He* will rule—not men for themselves, even as they abuse the name of His Love for their own purposes.

That is also why *He* determines the route by which His revelation will come to the enduring "heart" of transient man. That route travels *through* created reality, calling man to faith. All this takes place in and with the aid of history, through which man individually and communally, together with the rest of temporal creation, must pass. This means that it is of utmost importance to have a right view of the focal point of Revelation's application. That point cannot coincide with a temporal starting point. The Giver of revelation has ruled sovereignly over this revelatory creational history, but at all times He bound man to what He "*really*" had to say. Once more, therefore, the question arises as to the meaning of "*groundmotive.*"

We have already met with several formulations that represented different groundmotives. They were human formulations. They showed lingual, analytical, and historical aspects, to mention just these. None of them could reach deep enough to express the basic force they intended. Three of them—that of antiquity, the humanistic motive, and the motive of nature-supernature—originated from man. Each of them, more or less consciously, expressed man's idea of autonomy. Each time this autonomy dialectically called forth, from creation, a counter-pole that, in terms of this very autonomy, was both its tool as well as its counter instance. This dynamic dialectic is part and parcel of the confusion in the border zone. Its expression in theoretical language was the business of philosophy. These motives move life, and by moving life, move thinking, but there is no way to get behind them through thinking.

The question as to whether it is possible by human means to formulate the motive that in reality moves creation, and in doing so is revelatory, becomes now even more acute. There is a line of demarcation here, set up by the only Sovereign. Even so, from His side, in language we can understand, he threw *the* Light upon what He desired to make clear to us in His doings. That light was His only and all-decisive action for all history and all existence, *His* coming among us, His submersion in our ruin, and His victory.

13. Focal point of application

It follows that there is an important difference between understanding and comprehending. The groundmotive is given by God for man's "understanding." It is His earnest intention by which we shall live. But man cannot in his thinking get behind it so as to grasp or alter it. But he can falsify his understanding of it to serve the illusion of his own autonomy. This illusion was fostered under the guidance of the nature-supernature motivation, and not least of all by theology.

We have seen two schools, under cover of the mist of the border zone, wrestle with this big question: What is truly the moving force of creation? They were verticalism and reformational philosophy. Horizontalism, by contrast, sees no need to wrestle, because it claims to grasp what cannot be comprehended and ends up deciding for itself. It was met with the reaction of radical verticalism, which takes God's Rule to be the direct opposite of creation. Even though the latter is God's handiwork, creation as a result of the fall is definitely lost forever. However, our question is: How does verticalism know? *From what point* did it gain this insight?

Reformational philosophy, the second school, drew attention to the groundmotives and sought to show that dialectical groundmotives are untenable. Initially it formulated the biblical groundmotive as "creation-fall-redemption." This was intended to be according to the evident meaning of Scripture. Also, it was not a dialectical formulation, but meant to indicate an order of real occurrence.

How did we arrive at such "ordering" in our formulation of the fundamental moving force of our createdness? Our formulation was primarily directed against the dialectical motives of the opposition. Even though thinking helped in the search for it, it was not found *by* thinking. It was taken from the historical course of successive communications of Scripture. It did not lie on the level of theoretical thought itself, but below it, as an inner religious motivation, just like the motivating grounds of the conceptions opposed to it. Even so, it should not be forgotten that these religious motivations were most of all characterized by the basic, unprovable *faith* in theoretical thinking as the servant of human autonomy, whether pre-consciously as in antiquity, or consciously as in humanism. And so, against the backdrop of centuries of theology, the question must be asked: To what extent has human thinking also played a role in reformational philosophy's formulation of the biblical groundmotive? Is it possible that that particular role would have to be discontinued?

Here we have to ask the same question we asked with regard to radical verticalism: from what point would it be possible to gain insight into such an ordering? In their search for an answer to this question, both schools have relinquished basic trust in thinking reason. Verticalism tentatively refers to a condition or event from before the creation about which Scripture is not explicit, but yet possibly hints at in an obscure fashion. To this, we respond with a very straightforward question: Does God call believers to understand the only possible foundation for all understanding, namely nothing more or less than the cross of His Son, on the basis of such hints? Should we not be on our guard here that in spite of all our "good" intentions we might be calling God to account for His acts of Love? Are we sure that we do not harbor a deep desire to look behind the back of His intentions? Can this be the ultimate starting point for unreserved adoration? I believe that already in the Old Testament those who were called did receive the revelation and awaited its consummation *on the basis of* their entire *earthly life*. Their life *as revelation*, that is, not their life for its own sake, as horizontalism would have it. When its revelatory function has been fulfilled, this life will *perish*.

As a scientific enterprise Reformational philosophy is part of *this* life. By philosophical means it combats the pseudo-revelatory pretensions in philosophy. Via its "transcendental criticism," it draws attention to the groundmotives that lie beyond theoretical scrutiny. It confesses that its own groundmotive should only be based on Scripture. Therefore, understanding Revelation is its number one priority, even as such understanding can only be the understanding of faith, for without faith any understanding must remain barren with regard to confession and combat. We reaffirmed earlier that the God of revelation consigned creation to man in his history and that in *this* way He revealed Himself to us. That is why there *were* differences in the way Adam, Noah, Abraham, David, and the prophets were addressed, all the way to Zachariah and his son John—they were grounded in the earthly events and lives of these servants.

Should reformational philosophy—today—seek to start from the *beginning* of the *historical* line of revelation, or should it expect its dynamic, which it affirms to be the dynamic that moves creation, to come from the inner Origin of that revelation itself? I am convinced of the latter. And it does not have far to search, for the beginning of the Gospel of John indicates in no uncertain terms where the point of application for the understanding of creation is to be sought. We read there not only that the creative Word has become "flesh," but above all that we have beheld its "glory," glory as of the only Son from the Father. And this was

57

his glory: to be triumphant *through* the cross, for in his earthly appearance (in his suffering, that is) he had no form that we should look at him. That is the glory of the Creator Who bows down deep into the lostness of creation. That is the dynamics of creation and the only point from which we can understand its *revelatory meaning*. All the rest is arranged around *that*. There is no historical line, neither straight nor dialectically broken, that can show us the saving antithesis; a reality denied by horizontalism and sought above creation by verticalism. Only by beholding this "glory," hidden for the eye of the flesh, can we discover this saving antithesis. It is this glory alone that enables us to live up until the present day and that will maintain our life until the antithesis will be finished before our eyes. In following in His "dynamic" trail there will be no other glory for us.

14. Developing the "transcendental critique"

We have had to deal with much confusion in the "border zone." It was a confusion created by centuries of philosophical pseudo-revelation, most of the time operating by means of covert operations. Nowadays, with the pretense of avoiding this tumult, pragmatistic methodologism actually stretches the confusion to its limits. That is why we had to raise the question concerning the way in which Christians in general should try to find their own way in the midst of this uncertainty. But now we have to come to an assessment of the way in which reformational philosophy initially justified its entrance into this border zone.

Three things will have to be taken into account: in the first place, the historical setting of this initial confrontation; secondly, the fact that it sought engagement without a viable theory of structure; and thirdly, the lack of a fully developed account of the groundmotives. In particular, the structure and motivation of acts and actions along the tracks of time's dimensions, a matter of central importance, stood in need of deeper investigation. There had been no opportunity yet to deal with Heidegger's philosophy of time, nor with the modern consequences of positivism and with the modern but less than comprehensive attempts to deal critically with these consequences. It is true that after a while some questions were raised about the depth-perspective of reformational philosophy, but neither these questions nor the answers submitted adequately sounded that depth.

These questions had been raised in the hope of generating a discussion about the basics that could possibly contribute to revitalizing and correcting cooperation with and among the special sciences. It remains to be seen if these expectations were justified, especially if we take into account the elementary nature of the structure of theory and of the insight into the groundmotives that had been developed up to that point. There are no results that would confirm this expectation. In fact, there had been no attention at all given to the pseudo-revelatory nature of philosophy in the border zone. The main focus was initially limited to "theory," since it was believed that there was a fundamental difference between theoretical and non-theoretical thinking.

There was no doubt that thinking theoretically was all about acquiring knowledge. While it was assumed that in daily life adequate knowledge is gained via non-reflective thought, and while this "naive" thinking was supposed to cling somewhat passively to "sensory appearance," theoretical knowledge was conceived to be in need of a theory of knowledge. We have already touched on Hegel's opinion regarding this matter. Yet, in this context, his warning cannot be of primary concern for us. After all, his philosophical endeavors could only function against the backdrop of the Gegenstand relation presumed by the entire philosophical tradition from Descartes to Kant. After humanism became self-conscious about its supposed rational autonomy, there was simply no way of going back behind it. In fact, Hegel's depreciation of the priority of epistemology was intended to be a dialectical abolition of the restriction of "theoretical reason" by Kant and its subordination by Fichte. Still, neo-Kantianism intentionally revived the problem, claiming that it was not only significant for the knowledge of "nature."

Initially, the "Philosophy of the Cosmonomic Idea" described the specific character of theoretical "knowing" (as distinct from everyday intuition and thinking) as an opposition between actual thinking and its "Gegenstand." What it then regarded as the problem to be solved concerned the question of how knowledge is acquired via a synthesis between these two poles. As we saw before, the neo-Kantian answer was that this synthesis comes about from one pole, the pole of actual thought. In this way this one pole remained in the position of origin and root of rational reality, behind which it was not possible to go. The Philosophy of the Cosmonomic Idea called this the "archimedean point" and it continued to use this expression when it commenced its search for its own point of departure.

Naturally, we have to ask how far the analogy, implied by this term, was meant to go. Archimedes had intended a fixed point from which the earth could be moved. So, he meant it as his own fixed position. For humanistic *thinking*, this analogy was perfectly appropriate. Humanism thinks it can find a point, on this side of the "border," from where everything can be surveyed, comprehended, and connected. That this would be true can *not* be proven in or by thought. It is a basic conviction. There really is no other absolute point for Humanism than this actual "cogito."

That is why the Philosophy of the Cosmonomic Idea referred to another point, beyond all human functioning, the root from which all human functioning issues, and from which, consequently, the theoretical synthesis could be realized without being tossed between various competing basic denominators. It referred to Abraham Kuyper's idea of the inner religious point of concentration, called it the individual "heart" of man, and ascribed to it the status of the universal "root" of created reality. Thus far our comment on this conception has been deliberately incomplete. However, if we want to discuss the decisive significance of this idea for opposing the supra-theoretical conviction of reason's autonomy, then we first of all have to pay attention to the place from which we raise our questions (*der Ort des Fragens*). Where are we standing when we set forth our critical comments and questions? If we are not careful, we might find ourselves going astray "at the border" and wandering into metaphysical "territory."

The first decision we have to make concerns the place from which we begin our "questioning." Do we start from inside the sector of theory itself, where we met the axioms of humanistic thought, and where the Philosophy of the Cosmonomic Idea commenced its attack on the monopoly of the "cogito"? The Philosophy of the Cosmonomic Idea concentrated its argument on the question: Can we inquire behind the "cogito," yes or no? If not, then all "Gegenstände" that present themselves here are not only modally, but integrally, qualified by their relation to the cogito. However, the idea of the sphere-sovereignty of the theoretical sector only makes sense in as much as this sector cannot be reduced to any other sector. But relative to the "*radix*" of all that is, it simply loses its meaning.

Acknowledging an "archimedean point" for ourselves *within* the relatively sovereign sector of theory would be to suppose that it can serve as a connecting organ that provides us with an *overview* of *all* functions within that sector and their interrelations, "thinking" included. It would also be the organ to connect "thinking" with what is to be thought about. But such a point, on a par with and over against the "cogito" that we are bound to repudiate, *ties* us *down* to that sector.

However, the organ ("point") that the Philosophy of the Cosmonomic Idea proposed for this surveying and inter-connecting task was not on the same level as the "cogito." Rather, it appealed to Kuyper's doctrine about the central point from out of which all sectors of *life* take their issue. It is from that point that *all* activity, the activity within the sector of theory too, originates. It therefore has its "rank" "above" *all* activity and "above" *all* sectors of our existence. The question that now arises is: With such a difference in status, how is transcendental criticism possible? After all, on the one hand, such a criticism would involve a discussion, amid the "Gegenstände" in the theoretical sector, that is based on a "theoretical" equality with the originally theoretical "cogito" and that is guided by some ideal of a minimal mutual understanding. And yet, on the other hand, it takes its stance in a "point" from which all rival claims to competence must be rejected—notwithstanding that, as the history of Western civilization so evidently shows, it is precisely this claim to competence that is brought forward by the "cogito." Therefore, according to us, it is indeed a case of "either-or." Even while we do not desire to engage prematurely in transcendent criticism, it is here, we suspect, that transcendental criticism finds its (immanent) limits.

But there is more. The "cogito" (or "actual thinking," or however it may be called) is a product of human abstraction and reflection. It can without objection be termed a "point," even though it is wrongly viewed as an active agent. But this is surely *not* the case with the Radix of creation. There is no choosing of an ("archimedean") standpoint in the Radix. We are *driven* by the *radical dynamism* at work there, regardless of whether this is recognized or whether we try to resist it with the aid of something like the "cogito." However, in view of the confusion in the "border zone," this declaration by itself will not suffice. In reality, the abstract "cogito" is situated *within* the "temporal coherence" that pervades this zone. So, where in the relativity of time should we look for the universal Radix of creation that *drives* everything and that shows itself as radix precisely in as much as it imposes upon man the inevitable choice of the *direction* of his life's movement?

We must look for it only there where the Creator started his work, *before* time, at the beginning of the course of time, propelling things forward *in* time. We must not look for it in the confusing border zone, where pseudo-revelation all too quickly misled man. We must look for it "beyond," where any discussion based on an equality with the "cogito" is impossible and where it is proven to be in the wrong in all sectors of life, theory included. This is an assignment we have to pass on to all who carry responsibility in whatever area of life, each with its own "structure." The question for them is: Along which route will they receive their assignment in order to bring it to completion on "this side"? True, the structural routes for the theorist are proper to his sector, but as regards their structural order and their propelling driving force they are not different from the routes in other sectors. With attention for its own limitations and its own interconnections, it is up to each sector to actualize its connection with, and contribution to, the whole of life.

At this point we reach a juncture where a special level of attentiveness is required from everyone who actually has to labor in the fields of theory, but especially from those who have become accustomed to the primacy of theoretical reason. They are all equally influenced by the centuries-old deception of the supposed primacy of theoretical thought and its applications, including its applications in theology.

Before we can deal with this problematic, we will have to broaden the basis of transcendental criticism. We will have to do so according to the demands of the onward disclosure of philosophy, and in such a way that it will serve both the discussion with "horizontalism" and with a partial "verticalism." In what follows there will be several things that have also been dealt with in *Radix, Time, and Knowing* and in *Sign and Motive of Creation.*[6]

15. Knowing

We have to ask ourselves whether philosophy's progress around us has not led to a change in the understanding of and the appreciation for philosophy as such. Within classical humanism, starting from the pole of autonomy and via the polar oppositions in the 17th and 18th century, philosophy has continued to develop on into the era between the two great wars. Now it finds its definitive perspective in Heidegger's philosophy of Being. This philosophy is in fact a declaration of surrender. By contrast, positivism and pragmatism, joining forces in an exclusive methodologism, are riding high. But their original position as philosophies, albeit as "silent" philosophies, is being threatened from the outside—no longer by a dialectical attack in the name of the idea of autonomy, but by an attack from the side of the powers that were called forth from the religious seed-bed of this idea, namely *power* as such, accompanied by the fantasy of unrestrained "lust."

This is the inevitable result of pseudo-revelation in the Western world. For a time, following the fashion of the ancients, it was allied to "wisdom." But wisdom's task is finished since it became employed by various forms of "cognitive interests" (*Erkenntnis-Interessen*, Habermas).[7]

---

6 *Radix, Tijd en Kennen* (Amsterdam 1971) and *Teken en Motief der Creatuur* (Amsterdam 1965).

7 By alluding to Habermas's book *Knowledge and Interest*, Mekkes appears to be refer-

And even though, in the tension between the two current political power blocks, there is some renewed philosophical reflection in the wake of Hegel and Marx, this reflection actually documents the bankruptcy of philosophy, possibly even more clearly than does positivism. This kind of "Reflection" is sooner an *unmediated* realization of the actual historical developments. Philosophy's only task here is to scan, in passing, what is going on. It has to *grasp* the "material truth" (*Sachwahrheit*). Rüdiger Bubner expresses himself plainly: "Philosophy, which thus can be called a *theory* by which we *understand* our own *recognition,* continues to have, at most, a mediating influence on philosophizing subjects, and in no way can there be a direct theoretical influence any more of a theoretical account of things upon the real course of events in time; they never care in the least about philosophy."[8] In other words, for pseudo-revelation to have its effect, it no longer needs direct articulation and grounded understanding.

At this point it is necessary to return to Martin Heidegger as the representative of the other religious pole of humanism. He, from his side, actually said the same thing. Man is subject to time's disposition. "Presently necessary thinking" (*das jetzt nötige Denken*) taught him that Being had now once again sovereignly turned itself, namely towards revealing this message. The fate of the present time is the tyranny of technicistic pragmatism. We have no power over it whatsoever, neither philosophically nor in any other way, since it is determined by Being's disposition. For proud humanistic self-consciousness nothing is left but to "jump off."

Both of these positions are open to immanent critique—to analysis and assessment "from the inside-out." According to Heidegger's own conception, Being continuously and unceasingly turns and decides out of its own arbitrariness. But then, what would be the ground for concluding from such a transitory, albeit presently necessary thinking, that Heidegger's prophesying has any lasting universal validity? Likewise, if philosophy for no more than a moment reflects in order to formulate a "material truth" and to leave it subsequently to the stream of time, then how is it able amid the stream of time to validate precisely *this* reflective "understanding" (Bubner) as a *lasting* reality?

---

ring here to the pragmatistic turn, according to which knowledge is merely a tool in the service of practical interests (tr).

8   "Philosophie, die demnach begreifendes Erkennen und Theorie genannt werden darf, hat allerhöchstens mittelbar über philosophierende Subjekte und keineswegs in direkter Verantwortung der Theorie noch Einfluss auf die realen Zeitläufe, die sich um Philosophie nie scheren" (*Hermeneutik und Ideologiekritik* 1971, 243).

But with this immanent criticism, we are in no way done with our task. Quite to the contrary, it obliges us to account for the proper norm according to which we have to evaluate these antinomic depths. On superficial inspection we only notice the inner contradiction in the logical aspect of these two basic positions. Of course, these threatening contradictions did in no way escape the attention of its designers. That is why those who take "Reflection" in the sense of *im-mediate* conscious realization declare plainly that this reflection itself is taken up in the movement of time. And Heidegger tells us that he owes it to Being's turning *now* that he could both discern the inevitability of the technicistic disposition and "understand" the *present* near voice of Being that has thus decided.

In both cases, though logically no longer really possible, these are last attempts to give the final word to human *thinking* before the power "interest" forever does away with the "knowledge" concern. This entails a warning for those who are concerned that our philosophy would, by being preoccupied with what is going on here, fall short in its duties with regard to the special sciences. The combined power of science and praxis will meet with no resistance, if people with higher responsibility do not arm themselves from the depths where the real oppositions originate and from which science and praxis obtain their intellectual weaponry. It is rather easy to point out logical contradictions, but doing so will be of no avail when the opposition consciously reckons with the true extent of what is at stake here.

With all his philosophical experience, Heidegger would not have engaged in the fundamental antinomy just referred to, if he had not hit upon an absolutely intransgressible limit. It was *the* limit, the "border" that we have been meeting ever since the beginning of our investigation. It is the border where thinking is no longer to any avail and where our choices can no longer be *intellectually justified.* We have described theoretical activity, with philosophy in its defining center, as one sector of life. Of concrete life, and taken up by it. It was an image fit for our purposes then, but it has its limitations. It remains an abstraction from frozen motion. With the dynamics left out, it does not give us the most important indication that we all need.

Some, following as a matter of course in Hegel's trail, referred to pre-theoretical human consciousness as "reflection." In doing so, they at least touched upon the deep trail of "knowing." The later Heidegger regarded knowing as listening to Being. In this way, he had set in motion what, in his first period, he had called the hermeneutical point of application. Hermeneutical philosophy was then to start in "existence,"

in conscious and responsible "being there" (*Dasein*). We have recognized
the remainders of the "cogito" in this conception. But for Heidegger
it meant much more. For the first task of hermeneutical philosophy is
to account for life-choices, one of which is the theoretical occupation
with the frozen abstraction of "what is at hand" (*das Vorhandene*). But
existential responsibility with its everyday knowledge, implied in life's
choices, far exceeds theory. Only by taking this excess into account will
it be possible to arrive at a comprehensive hermeneutical understanding
of the meaning of temporal existence; even though the ultimate depth of
meaning is but reached in authentic knowing, by the "call of conscience"
(*Anruf des Gewissens*).

We do not need the admonitions of these examples in order to be
convinced of the dynamic movement of our existence. Thinking, both
in daily life and in theory, as well as the knowing that pervades our lives,
are all part of it. But the question urges itself upon us even more: Should
we, for the sake of a transcendental critique that was designed to make
thought-contact, continue to put a "theory of knowledge" up front amid
the confusions in the "border zone"? We explained this question when we
dealt with "*der Ort des Fragens.*"

Here we give our answer. We say, "No!" Those with whom we wanted to establish or to continue communication understood that we do not
disregard the difference in the *level* of our respective "starting-points."
The problem was that we did not adequately realize the depth of the distinction between the root of the cosmos and individual existence on the
one hand and choosing an "archimedean point" in the sector of theory
on the other.

The philosophical pseudo-revelations of the West have pretty much
played out their evolution and mutual polar tensions. There was a last effort by the *Frankfurter Schule* to throw up something of a rampart against
the overwhelming flood of the *powers* to which all theoretical thought has
become subservient. But all along the line, in what was formally the humanistic camp, Nietzsche's insight prevailed. He had raised his prophet-
ic-philosophic voice. Then, continuing within the tradition of Western
philosophy, Heidegger thought Nietzsche's prophecy through to its end.
Positivism and pragmatism, surfacing in the 19th century and reinforced
by linguistic analysis in the 20th century, have turned their back on the reflections of Kierkegaard, Nietzsche, and Heidegger and have become the
theoretical promoters of that practice of life the consequences of which
these three thinkers had foreseen. Today Western philosophy has nothing
more to say. It remains to be seen what the East will have to offer in the

future. For the time being, it feeds on the fruits of Western praxis and science, whose influence, in spite of all efforts to prove the contrary, cannot be understood apart from the philosophical insights that have nourished them. So, let us be somewhat more emphatic: what has been the actual (life-)function of these insights? Our answer was that they functioned as "pseudo-word-revelation." That is to say that, as basic insights beyond critical scrutiny, they intended to *direct* all of human life and human experience. In so doing, they deployed a force that could only have been derived from creational dynamics, for its effect can in no way be explained if they had been mere theoretically secured insights.

Naturally, this is true for reformational philosophy as well. The difference, however, lies in its decisive declaration that it is open to all probing behind it, that it is itself part of creation, and that it can give its insight into the development of creation only by reference to the Word that called creation into being and that carries it to its destination. That is why, as philosophy, it stands in principle, and now also historically, in solidarity with the rest of Western philosophy at the limiting border of what human thought can reach. That is why its primary duty is to think about that "border." This duty first of all implies that, in the confusion of the border zone, it equally oppose those who *in fact* deny the "other side," as well as those who, theologically or otherwise, are of the opinion that they can take their starting point for a theoretical advance from yonder side *as such*. What it needs to find in order to help point the way to the straying Western mind is the *point of application* for *its* hermeneutics. This it will find in *the* Word revelation (see Isaiah 53 and John 1). Apart from *this*, there is no way and no perspective, neither here nor there.

16. Norm, time, and structure

In order to reduce the possibility of misunderstanding, I will from here on no longer refer to the "Philosophy of the Cosmonomic Idea." I used this designation above because some of its characteristic emphases have contributed to its recognition and remain worthy of mention. But from now on I will speak of "reformational philosophy" in order to indicate as clearly as possible *the* point from which all-that-is has its origin, namely, the "Word" with which the gospel of John begins and that, according to this revelation, was and remains *the* Beginning.

This is of such universal significance that for reformational philosophy to say what it has to say, there is no *primary* need for a term like "creation" in the sense of a determining "law." The primary meaning of the term "law idea" was another one. It was meant to indicate that human *knowing*, especially theoretical and philosophical knowing, is bound *to* the given order *for* knowing by which its meaning is determined and of which it is to give an account, either implicitly or explicitly. The content of this inevitable account was called "law idea." It was to be the first subject of inquiry in the dialogue with the philosophies that claimed to be autonomous but that nonetheless proved to be very much bound to this order.

Secondly, in developing its theory of structures, reformational philosophy used the term "law" to indicate the determination, beyond all human arbitrariness, of—created—"structures." Of course this determination was beyond doubt, just as in its transcendental criticism it was beyond doubt that human knowing is determined by its given structure.

From its very inception, reformational philosophy emphasized the dynamic character of creation, for this dynamics is the primordial revelation of God to the creature. That is what it meant when it spoke of the ground*motive* of creation. As creation's basic dynamics, it cannot but manifest itself in the apostate motives of "pseudo-revelation" as well.

Earlier we had to consider the question: Can we give a name to our own groundmotive by starting from a historical beginning of the line of revelation? Or can we rather only approximate it from the dynamic Center of God's revelation, which we have now received "in these last days," in contrast to it being passed down from "of old" (Hebrews 1)? We answered that the latter is the case, and we cannot emphasize this too much. But then we have to be more careful with how we use the word "law."

We have seen the end of the law, its "fulfillment," and we have witnessed its "completion," realizing that through the law we died unto the law. We can no longer look at creation as though there had been no fall and death, but neither can we regard creation as subject to *eternal* death. From this perspective the confusion in the border zone appears to be extreme. If we think we have understood anything at all of this Center from which all is fulfilled, then we can no longer try to piece together a perspective about the ordering of the cosmos on the basis of the idea of "creational law." We have to live in, for, and unto Him Who died and was raised for us. One thing has yet to happen to our temporal "creation": its vanishing. Until then, it will have to stand as witness and tool of God's favor. He has sustained it in its structures to that end, but these structures are dynamic and they can only unfold their true meaning in dynamic direction towards Him *Who is coming.*

They can in no way be cut off from Him, neither by treason, nor by neglect, nor by (possibly well-intended) denial. Horizontalism is directly offensive to His offer here below. "Verticalism," however well-intended, underestimates the power of His resurrection. If we think that we can in any way resolve matters with a "horizontal" dimension of structures we simply exchange the foggy twilight in the border zone for the deep of night. And if we think that we can leave the night behind by merely looking to the "beyond," we are time and again entangled in endless antinomies. For every tool that we use, every word, every image, our reasoning and our inspiration, all these are taken from this "side"—as were the Master's own words and parables, the comfort and encouragement He gave, even the demonstration materials of His miracles. So too, He preferred to be laid in the grave "on this side," *in order* from *there* to be raised.

Therefore, it is impossible to speak of creational ordinances as something in themselves. In its vigilance against the nature-supernature motive, as well its temporary corollary, the common-grace motive, reformational philosophy has always rejected such a construction. Something completely different is meant by the term "structures." Structures are confirmed under the rainbow, but it is precisely the rainbow that indicates their dynamic fulfillment. Structures did prepare the way for the Victor, but after His victory they were not meant to continue to go before Him, but rather to follow after Him.

This is what "motivates" them, even when apostate motivation uses them to direct human experience in the opposite direction. They are motivated along the track of time. And it is here that we see a specific task for reformational philosophy. Refusing the invitation of each and every autonomy, it *follows* the structures by *seeking* their meaning, not by any light of reason, but by reason enlightened by integral Truth through *faith*. Here lies the decisive difference between every profession of self-sufficient thinking and the deep significance of the expression "structure of time." "Structures" have their place between motivation and time.

Time is the *track* of motion of the ever-motivated creational dynamics. The original motivation was God's act of creation. This act was *directed* and *focused*. In the course of creation's time, that focus was to be revealed as the center of God's intentions. The Old Testament revelation, in its history and in the prophetic words that came with it, already abounds with warnings not to look for any basic intention apart from the one to be shown in the fullness of time. The preaching of the One sent by God continued revelation in this way and made it reach its climax. If we want to look for a more basic intention, we violate the Glory of the Word from the beginning, no matter if we desire to do so out of pretended wisdom or in an attempt to defend God's dealings. We may even try to do so in our desire to raise the confusion in the border area of pseudo-revelation by marking the antithesis in time—but which in fact would amount to an attempt to take control of the "border." God's Word is the alpha and omega of His intention. Sovereignly it draws everything to the completion defined by itself. The deformity of the unrecognized King (Isaiah 53) was, and remains, integral to the—spiritual—"glory" shown by the Gospel.

There is no way to identify the Origin with the Radix of creation, but even less can they be divorced from one another. In the Son of his love God showed Himself openly, and thereby revealed His deepest being and intentions to us, while from our side the beginning of revelation is our own temporal experience. How far we humans, in receiving His revelation, will be able to reach during our lifetime depends on the date and the period of our "being there," the location where we live, the ear we give to revelation, and the direction and intensity of our inner and outer experience. *All of this* is what "structure" is about. And as far as people refusing or following is concerned, let us not forget the warning implied in: "What have I to do with judging others? Doing so is God's business." Every inquiry into this matter that reaches beyond the imposed limits reaches back behind "the beginning of revelation" and *is* thereby "judged."

Meanwhile, one distinction is of paramount importance, especially today, namely between "law" and "subject." This correlation needs to be clarified of course, especially after what we just said about the meaning of "law." But without a clear understanding of it, we cannot deal with "structure." Today, structure usually refers to a certain coherence of actually existing elements. The more often some definite coherence is encountered, the more justified it appears to refer to such coherence as a "structure." The concept of a structure is constructed from elementary components, after which the components found in a recurring complex are tested against this construct or possibly classified differently. Clearly, this way of looking at things is fashioned after the method of the natural sciences and conditioned by the *power* of the "silent philosophy" in the background, namely, the positivistic-pragmatistic world-and-life-view.

When we, in contrast, want to understand "structure" only against the background of the law-subject correlation, we do not mean to give priority to some fixed concept of law. Nor do we intend to replace the natural sciences' concept of law with another concept. We are happy to learn from the natural sciences how the concept "natural law" evolved, realizing that here too this concept is increasingly losing its formerly fixed character. Yet we take it that this does not hold the prospect of approaching some solid bottom about which we can give a gradually more scientific account. Rather, it signposts an unfathomable depth of *structure*.

In contrast to today's generally accepted Western scientific approach to things, we do *not* expect a common basis for discussion to come from a positivizing theory of science. The areas of life that extend beyond "nature" should not be approached in analogy with natural science, but the reverse, the employment and the study of "nature" should take place in dependence on what transcends nature. Each science has its own sector and method. However, ultimately even the mutual relations between the methods of the sciences have to express the totality of the cosmic order. That is why the question regarding the possibility and impossibility of an "archimedean point" is important *for science* internally. But we also understand that the importance of theory is merely partial and that the entire theoretical sector of life is dependent on the reality dynamics in the *root* of creation.

The mutual coherence of the various domains of life is rooted in this original dynamics, which is reflected in theoretical thought. But a mere reflection of this orderly coherence is not enough. It is to be taken explicitly into account in the way theoretical thought organizes itself. Our discriminating discernment of this order, and our willingness to take it into account, depend on our integral and "radical" insight into the *meaning* of creation *as* "creation." Given the positivistic times in which we live, this insight is crucial. For all of these reasons, the concept of "structure" comes to shoulder a comprehensive significance in which the correlation of law and subject together with the mutual modal order within the coherence of time should show us the way. This is not a matter of theoretical schematics, but a matter of decisive *principle*.

17. Creational dynamics vs. present thinking[9]

Martin Heidegger's fame is first of all due to his modern metaphysics of Being in the wake of his earlier hermeneutical philosophy of existence. In his final period the temporal movement of "Being," or Being's disposition in time, came to have the "last word." We pointed out the internal antinomy that is involved here, and we showed that it was inevitable. There was no other way left for Heidegger to philosophize, for he had met with "the" border. At the same time, little is left for the modern-humanistic counter-pole of pragmatism but to cower behind the blinds

---

9   See note 2.

of the "theory of science," possibly supplemented by a theory of language in a Freudian sense. None of this, however, takes away from the significance of the border that Heidegger had confronted.

In *Radix, Time, and Knowing* we tried to show that he had to confuse two "horizons," namely, the horizon of theory and the horizon of time. His philosophy, pretending to speak its "word" with final universal validity, had claimed that the ultimate horizon for all philosophy was what it had itself said about (Being's) time. But that very "final" word remained a philosophical word, that is to say, a theoretical word. Theory was Heidegger's ultimate trust. Given his *faith* in this pseudo-revelation this was all he could come up with. Here lies the origin of his antinomic construction. That being said, we have to take into account that for Heidegger, that is to say *in* his philosophy, theoretical thinking was relegated to a secondary position, so he will in no way be able to accept our description. For him, the philosophical view transcends theory, while for us it is and remains "theooria"[10] throughout all the phases of its development.

In truth, what Heidegger really did was to speak metaphysically-theoretically about "time." For positivism such speaking is an abomination, while for natural science it is per definition beyond the meaning of each of its disciplines. The actual situation is that each special science can only work with a "concept" of time, the meaning of which is, in every case, dependent upon the place that that concept assumes within that science. A theoretical "idea" of time remains a universal concept or, more precisely: it simply is not possible. This leaves only a residual concept of a *measure* of time to work with in the sciences.

So, Heidegger's confusion of horizons indicates that, for him, it is not possible to look beyond (in our sense) theoretical *thinking*. For us it is not possible to look beyond *time*. That is to say, *thinkingly* it is not possible!

Thus, it is incumbent upon us to account for what is at stake when we talk about time and its horizon. It is not the *measurement* of time that puts us *in touch* with time. We *are* in touch with time through the impassable reality of human temporal duration. "Duration" is not meant here in the Bergsonian sense of "durée" as the basic denominator of reality. Yet we recognize the depth of Bergson's insight. For it is indeed man who by his experience and his account thereof is called to understand *the* meaning of all existence. And this is an ongoing task throughout the generations. The metaphysical "uno intuitio" is in no way granted to

---

10 "θεωρία" (theory) is what Plato puts forward as the better vehicle to approach the race of the gods, better than "opinion" or "belief" (tr).

man. What he needs is the duration of his life, for in the course of history the point of accountability is ultimately to be found in each man's individual life—normally, a good number of decades, according to the solar *measure* of time. Within that time-span, the horizon of time becomes a reality for the individual man and thus for humankind. Here too, in human temporal duration, we find the integral meaning of the substrata of nature; for the internal motion in the cells of man's body are related with the revolutions of the heavens in an unfathomable cosmic coherence. For man's cosmic awareness the horizon of time is the final and furthest horizon of all that lives and exists. It is the horizon of creational revelation. The "beyond" of this horizon, the "eternal" as it is called by the creative Word, can in no way be reached from within time. As far as a "beginning" is concerned, there is only one Beginning, exclusively pointed out to us by the Word itself. It is the *only possible* starting point for our gaze. And there is only one "End" pointed out for our earthly gaze. The horizon defined by this Beginning and this End was endowed with meaning by the Word's bodily living *here,* in our flesh. Everyone who objects that this would amount to a form of "christomonism," betrays the fact that instead of listening exclusively to the revealing Word, he has positioned himself in some "archimedean point." In other words, he attempts with his mortal rationality to peep into a supposed "supernature."

The horizon of time is really given, but it is by no means a static given. The term horizon itself brings this to expression. For an horizon is what it is *for* those who face it and proceed in the direction it indicates. Into its *direction.* . . . Direction presupposes movement, and every movement—be it in a "literal" sense, as in the movement of physical energy, or in a more than physical sense—*is* only what it is as an expression of the all-encompassing and fundamental creational dynamics. For man, creation's movement takes place within the horizon of *time.* Put differently, as we saw before: the movement of creation's dynamics is along the *track* of time. The track is there due to this dynamics while history is its spoor. And the question is: "What is the deepest, basic meaning of creation's dynamics?" As we have noted already, the "structures," in their "law" sides as *giving* meaning and in their "subject" sides as realizing meaning, have their place between the motivation of creational dynamics and its regulation along the track of time.

Naturally, the track itself has its structure. It suits the *direction* indicated by the dynamics of creation. There is a beginning, a continuous advance, and a fulfillment. It has been denied to man to "know" the beginning, even as no one knows of the day and hour of time's fulfillment. But the right direction in the advance is for man's responsibility to choose. There is no way for him to withdraw from the advance, nor to excuse himself by an appeal to his "past" or to what he supposes to be decided about the future and its fulfillment. But while man has to search for the road he has to take, the direction has been shown to him by the Word.

Time imposes forward movement. It is the first thing that announces itself in every life. What counts is *how* we realize our responsibility in that forward movement. So, it is important to understand that the "horizon" of time is not like some fog hanging over the future, as though it were some terminal natural catastrophe. Of course, "horizon" is a metaphor, derived from nature. The natural horizon shows itself due to the vaulting of the dome of the skies over the globe, opening up the components of "horizontal" distance and height. Similarly, the philosophical metaphor alludes to the inevitable forward movement and the corresponding "how" of our responsibility in it.

Thus, it is *time* that offers the possibility and the framework for the structures. In each of the structures, the *dynamics* of time comes to expression. In the natural aspects of reality, subjectivity can only follow the track of time as defined by the "laws" of nature. But in the normative aspects, human responsibility is decisive. This is not to say that man can hold up the dynamics of time in any of these aspects. Under the normative aspects, there is no other option but to choose a direction, but there is the possibility here to choose against the norm. Which is what humankind did. In principle it responded and acted *against* the impulse and the direction of the Word from the beginning.

If reformational philosophy is to conform to the conditions of its initial choice, it will first of all have to reflect upon the priority of this original dynamics. Many of its early adherents were attracted by its sys- tematic framework, which they thought would enable them to meet with scientists of other persuasions on equal terms. There was, however, a typically scholastic familiarity with static methods of comparison at play here. Even though the "Philosophy of the Cosmonomic Idea" did break through these methods, the basic habit of thought, rooted in a longstanding theory of static forms of reason, was by no means dispensed with. The important theory of the "opening-process" was all too often treated as an addition, a movement to be added to a primary static order, *setting* the latter in motion, so to speak. From this followed the intense search for sediments of the movement (the retrocipations and anticipations, etc.) and the idea that it would be possible to speak about time otherwise than as the inevitably continuing track of the inevitably continuing movement, in which at every moment the decision lies in the choice of direction. This was in fact a serious underestimation of the power of reformational philosophy that then stood in the way of the benefits it had to offer. Each and every remnant of such restraining influence has to be dispensed with and that right quickly. The dynamics of creation is the dynamics of God's long-suffering, but it stretches "with haste" towards the fulfillment, the fulfillment of the glory of the Resurrection.

"Structure," as determined by fundamental motivation and time's regulation, can only be dealt with *after* we have emphasized the priority of time's dynamics and man's responsibility. Next comes the general order of the modal aspects that is expressed in *all* "structures." And only then can we deal with structures separately. This is indeed how it was done in "De Wijsbegeerte der Wetsidee" ("The Philosophy of the Law Idea," the initial Dutch title, which became *A New Critique of Theoretical Thought*). This order is quite appropriate in the light of the fact that in the theoretical sector of life, we are bound to the norms for systematic analysis and synthesis. Hence it is to be expected that the specific findings of science are crucial for determining the order in which we learn about the "modalities" and their mutual differences and similarities as well as their coherences. It is philosophy's task to describe the order of the modal structures comprehensively. The way in which it will fulfill this task depends upon its insight into the origin and root of what is. How reformational philosophy went about this task has been known for years. There has been secondhand abuse of its method and findings, for which it has been mocked. But the proper use of it is, first of all, to serve the critical enquiry into how pseudo-revelatory theories have falsified the scientific view of the world and of creation. Our primary target is the dialectics of the various absolutized basic denominators in which these pseudo-revelations get entangled. Such a focus intends to open peoples' eyes to the true Radix of our given reality, from which its dynamics originates and to which it is directed.

But there is no way that choosing the right direction can ever be the result of theoretical thinking. Theory is always restricted to one sector of the totality of life. The right choice, also in matters of theory, can only follow in the wake of the central choice of life in the root of personal existence. We will have to investigate how this choice works itself out, how dynamics and direction are concretized. Next we have to deal with the structures, using what we know about the modalities and their mutual coherence. It should be noted that this explanation does follow the order of systematic theoretical analysis.

74

With this last remark we immediately find ourselves in the midst of the dynamic reality that we are concerned with and of which we ourselves are a part. In systematic theoretical exposition the elements that we abstract from this dynamic reality are set apart in their mutual order. When we then try to account for the movement from which they were taken, we find that this movement, in its turn, becomes an element that we confront in our actual thinking. But thinking (a verb) is always fully actual. Thus, the theoretical confrontation takes place by observation of the "elements" *within* the actuality of thinking. Hence, it is only possible to speak of a so-called "opposition" of Gegenstände *over against* thinking in a secondary reflection. We have come across this before [Hegel, tr.]. This means that during the entire activity of thinking, a conscious and directed control of its actualization has to take place. This actual control is entirely enclosed within and motivated by the dynamics of creation; only in this way is it possible. Theoretical thinking can only facilitate this control by acting in such a secondary role, in which the same demand is repeated, again and again. The totality of this actuality is, together with all other actuality, taken up within an a priori "knowing," to which we shall return below.

In order to understand this state of affairs, we will have to break with most of the well-established traditions of Western rational control, namely the traditions that can be characterized by the expression "*present thinking*" (actual cogito). In recent years, assisted by the philosophical focus upon being and time, there has been some reaction against these traditions, even if it is far from a bold and principled reaction. This was extensively dealt with in *Radix, Time, and Knowing*. Here it is important to point out the consequences that follow from the rejection of these ("present thinking") traditions.

In metaphysics "present thinking" was conceived as thinking-of-being. It was taken to be the supratemporal "essential form" of man and conceived as perfect divine thinking in "ideas." Man's conceptual form-thinking was supposed to grasp the (measure or number of the) moments of the movement of time into a unity. The present moment became explicit in the humanistic conception of the "cogito," the actuality and the result of which could in each successive moment, again and again, be considered and corrected by the same "cogito."

The "cogito" was conceived to be operative in the "Gegenstand relation" (itself the construction of abstractive reflection). It could, again in a metaphysical manner, be invested with other functions (cf. Descartes, Locke, Romanticism, Hegel, Dilthey, the philosophy of existence). This line of thought came to a climax in the experiment-based natural sciences. From there it was completely emancipated and suprascientifically absolutized in positivistic pragmatistic methodologism. It was and remained itself an *abstraction* posited by abstractive thinking. In complete negation of anything that could possibly reach deeper, it was invested with a dignity that was nothing less than divine and that was regarded as the ultimate origin beyond which no inquiry was possible. Its proclamation of truth, whenever it was set forth, depended in each case upon the latest, and as such the most perfect, thinking at the latest actual moment.

After Husserl had brought the "cogito"-philosophy to the limits of its (im)possibility, his pupil Heidegger, following Kierkegaard and Nietzsche, had to wrestle with this problem. We have already met with the inevitable frontier against which the humanistic-religious basic dialectics had to run aground. In their turn the thinkers of *Knowledge and Interest* (*Erkenntnis und Interesse*, the Frankfurt philosophers) now run aground against the dialectics of their "dialectics" (in their narrower sense) and continued positivism. This is the end of the Western struggle for theoretical power. From now on the issue will be *power* as such. Science, from now on, will be a mere tool to be *used* in the struggle for power.

All of this testifies to the fundamental lie that is involved in the absolutization of the cogito. It also demonstrates the decline of all humanistic ideology. Humanism carved out a trail of power in which it would henceforth be drawn forward. There is possibly no clearer demonstration of what we mean by "structure" than this course of events. Scientific practice is being performed by theoretical "thinking," the exercise of power is performed by the *will* to control with all available means, legitimate or not. Then, *within* scientific practice, power shows itself as a compelling influence upon thinking from the outside: the power of the ancient form-matter motive and of the humanistic motive of autonomy and control. The deliberate attempt to *make use* of science is also driven by the pursuit of *power*, be it political or economic. In all these cases "power" shows its own original modality, the "historic" modality as reformational philosophy would have it. Here we are in the middle of the problem of the *structures*. Indeed, it is a problem that concerns their place between man's dynamic original motivation and the dynamics of time.

The dynamics of creation is potentially present in all of its modalities. It becomes actual in the totalities that are motivated by it and that manifest themselves in an endless variety of creational configurations. Since the two configurations we have mentioned here—Western thinking and historic power formation—are themselves already structured modalities *of* concrete individual structures, the question urges itself upon us as to where we, as creatures concretely subject to *being* created, will have to take our stance in order to discern something of these structures.

In the light of all that has gone before, it is clear that there is only one way, namely to take the direction shown by the central dynamics of creation. It is this central dynamics that moves us forward in our experience of the structures. In order to discern them according to their real meaning, we will have to let ourselves be taught by the Original Word. Only in this way will it be possible to live consciously and responsibly.

18. Dynamics, knowing, direction

It is necessary to explain this in more detail. There simply is no opportunity for *us* humans to "take a stance." The centuries-old idea of "present thinking" suggests that we can choose an archimedean "point"—our "own" (theoretical) consciousness—in order to survey from there what surrounds us. But once we have understood that we have been placed in the dynamics of our existence, and that we are thereby already motivated, then we know that (1) we *are* on the move, (2) that we are bound by the initial direction of our lives, and (3) that for the realization of our human lives we are to give responsible *direction* to this dynamic drive. We can only understand that we have this responsibility as God's image bearers once we set ourselves in the *right* direction, that is, when we *desire* to actualize the true dynamics.

Once more we find ourselves in the heat of the battle between Revelation and pseudo-revelation. For us to take an archimedean "stance" in order to see more than the humble revelation of the creative Word-made-flesh, even if this would be facilitated by "orthodox" theology, cannot but annihilate the only movement that opens our perspective for us. With such a "stance," the place of the "Creator" becomes untraceable, *our* fall becomes an accusation of impotence addressed at Him, and our salvation-*by-Him* is turned into our *own* "ethical" law experience and our *own* affective mystical experience. – *This* is eternal life that they *know* You. . . .

From early on the Western mind has been impregnated by a tradition that identifies "knowing" in its deepest, all-encompassing sense with θεωρία, the perfect (divine) thinking-of-being. In this tradition, the knowing in "Now this is eternal life: that they may know you" (John 17:3) is construed as "Christian" (theoretical) "idea-knowledge." Horizontalism would take it as ethically absolutized knowledge; its counterpole would take it as mystical knowledge. But what this prayer of Jesus in *truth* indicates is *the* direction of creational dynamics as it originates from its Radix, the suffering "Servant of the Lord." The way of created reality is not to be found apart from communion with His suffering. To *know* is to know *this* communion, not as if it belonged to "supernature," but as all-encompassing and all-impregnating. In service to this knowing *and from a far distance* theoretical knowledge may play its role in history, for a time. But this *central* knowledge comes first. *From out of* it comes the knowledge of structure, which is a necessary pre-condition of practical life. And only then comes theoretical knowledge. In fact, philosophy and its differentiation into the sciences came about via this necessary structural knowledge. But Western man has religiously interchanged what came first with what came last, so that now he is faced with a reality in which a reasonable account of power is no longer possible.

This central "knowing" rises to consciousness in our experience of the structures, which is the way in which we become responsible. Positivism turns this state of affairs upside down. It takes theoretical laboratory experience by itself for an absolute source of knowledge—the most modern "cogito." Methodologically it makes knowledge of "the facts" into the "norm," and by giving knowledge of nature precedence over every other kind of knowing, it requires that the latter be either sidelined or recast analogously. But in doing so, it effectively subjects man, who is meant to bear responsibility in freedom, to the tyranny of what is in fact his (scientifically orchestrated) *substratum*. Likewise, the true meaning of history is repudiated. Positivism explains history by means of "synchronic" and "diachronic" coordinates. And although there have been occasional, and since Dilthey ever more, attempts on the part of historicism to compensate for this meaninglessness by appealing to the general concept "coherence of action" (*Wirkungszusammenhang*), this really has not clarified very much at all.

Faced with the attempt of modern materialism, pragmatistic positivism, theological horizontalism, and neo-marxism to subject humankind to this substratum, we do not want to escape the problems of temporal life with a speculative grasp at "yonder side." Rather, we want to take life seriously in its earthly character, as regulated by time. Yet we do not want to let ourselves be pushed into what appears to yield temporal power in matters of life and death, but which would, a priori and intentionally, exclude the only meaning of life that can be truly *known*.

Whether he wants to or not, man knows. For the root of creation drives him to actualize such structures as are necessary for the maintenance of his life. Whether his knowing will take the right direction and will lead to truthful realization of these structures depends on the central choice he makes. Logical "pretheoretical" distinctions as based in the functioning of his organs and senses are no more than means to support his conscious knowing. Human knowing does not begin with nature, but with the orientation in his emerging self-consciousness. Underlying all that comes with the successive stages of human maturation and the pedagogical questions or methods connected with them is man's involuntary vital search for integral direction in his rapport with his being-there.

Man has to find this direction on his own, but the right direction that truly makes him *human* is determined by the Origin of his being in the world. So how do we get from this side, through the confused and confusing border zone, to true "knowing"? We do not come to know love or beauty or economics or our mother tongue through theoretical analysis. Such knowledge only comes by actually loving, by experiencing beauty's allure, by exchanging our experiences with others, and so on. All theorizing about these things is secondary, or even less than that. How then does a person truly learn to live? By what route does this all-encompassing and all-directing knowing get to the Truth?

As we have indicated, this route goes via the structures of time, and via the time of the structures. The structures are dynamic structures along the track of time. They are creatively regulative and given to man to be actualized. Our first responsibility, therefore, is to seek them as they are intended, that is to say, as directed to Him, in whose image we are made. In this way, along the track of time and by taking direction, we are to come to our destination.

Along the track of time and together with his contemporaries, man is awarded "seventy or eighty years," following upon the times and accomplishments of previous generations. If we knew no more than this, then despite all supernature-horizontalism, there would be no "horizon" for us at all. But we know of more, for in fact the horizon of time does present itself to us, stirring us to realize the meaning of our existence. It is precisely for that reason that all "materialism," even in Feuerbach's and Marx's humane treatment of it, is basically a lie from hell. This is plain from the satanic brutality with which the materialistic myth, propagated today by churches, etc., is engaged in the service of revolutionary dictatorships. We just referred to it as the tyranny of the substratum-belief. It rapidly clarifies and sharpens the antithesis in the world. Faithful philosophizing has to forcibly oppose this ultimate pseudo-revelation.

In *Radix, Time, and Knowing* we discussed the *dimensions* of time extensively. We showed that without taking them into account, no hermeneutics will be able to meet its goal. Man will not understand his course through history apart from these dimensions. For what matters is not the passage of time as measured in years or centuries, or the succession of facts and cultures. We are not concerned merely with ascertaining what prior generations wanted to express or accomplish. What counts is: Have earlier generations helped our generation look in the right direction? Or have they, and to what degree, led humanity astray from its destination? That is why the historistic terminology of "coherence of action" is confusing and extremely superficial. It does not get us any further than looking for what *has* happened. But it fails utterly when the historian would want to understand the *meaning* of what has happened.

We have called the structures of reality structures of time. They can only be realized in the actual *course* of time, i.e., through exercising—modal historical—power. While the modalities as such have their own universal "structure," they are meant and fit to be actualized in and through the structures of things and events. These structures are identified by the specific order of their modalities. The "Philosophy of the Cosmonomic Idea" called them individuality structures, and even while it always recognized the universal order of the modalities and the dynamics at work in them, it would be better to say that the modalities have their sole *reality in* this dynamics. But there is another, more urgent question to be considered here. It needs our focused attention. From which perspective must we begin our investigation of these various structures of individuality?

The natural structures are given to us. But over the course of history we realize other structures—some lasting others fleeting, weighty or modest, objectively imposing or subjectively mighty, while some unpretentious structures may be quite indispensable. The effectiveness of this historical power formation is striking. Initially it served in reformational philosophy as an example of how the formation of individuality structures is related to the structure of the modalities. Be that as it may, *everything* that exceeds nature both needs formation by man and at the same time also conditions the formation of individual and communal human life.

We have been emphasizing that the dynamics of creation arises and takes direction from out of its root, that this root is beyond the purview of every science, and that this dynamics both drives man forth in his responsibility and, on the other hand, invites him in his acts and his actions to choose direction. Therefore, our investigation of the structures of individuality will have to start with these acts and actions, for it is through them that we make our decisions and carry them out. Every individual man takes part here, depending on the relationships of responsibility in which he finds himself. We live and experience in and through our (inner) acts and (externalized) actions, while our responsibility in all this always and in the first place concerns our choice of *direction*.

Here we meet with the mutual ordering and dynamic inter-relationships of the modalities. We found an example of this in the relation between analytically qualified scientific thought and historically qualified power. The dynamic "opening"-process closes down, however, as soon as, with an eye to scientific control but with inevitable concessions to reality, we try to bring the variety of structures under one basic modal denominator. The questions that arise at this point are: What guides the development of the power that closes things down? and What guidance must human power follow in order for creation to open up? Either process will *start* in the same direction, simply because within creation there is no other possibility. But *where* is the decision being made concerning either opening up creation's meaning or cutting off its destination, with all the negative repercussions ensuing from that?

Clearly, it is in the heart of responsible man, in his decision for or against an orientation towards "yonder side." His existence is bound to earthly time and by earthly structures, so the question is: how is he nonetheless able either to choose his direction in accordance with creation's dynamics, or to consciously reject it? The answer is that the decision about the realization of structural norms is made in the *second* dimension of time, the so-called transcendental dimension.[11]

As we saw before and amply discussed in *Radix, Time, and Knowing*, without this dimension there would not really be a horizon at all. Still, we cannot but experience time as a horizon, while that is, moreover, the first and foremost condition for us if we are to discover *meaning* in existence. The horizon of time is the primary witness against the pretensions of "present thinking." That is why humanism refuses to recognize it and why modern nature-supernature thinking wipes it out it in its theology of the level plane, the (mathematical) plane without horizon.

The horizon calls. While we cannot look beyond it, its direction still implies an impetus to "get going." We take our direction by making our

---

11 The first "dimension" of time could also be called the "natural" dimension; the dimension that Mekkes calls the substratum (*Teken en motief der creatuur*, Amsterdam 1965, p. 185). It should be noted that both of these dimensions are also called "directions"—whereas time has but one direction, namely towards the future. But given the instruction that we are here concerned with "directions" of the time-order (H. Dooyeweerd, *A New Critique of Theoretical Thought* II, 76), the distinction seems clear (tr).

advance in measurable time subservient to a dimension that is not open to measurement. Then our quest for a "survey" will be met, even though no referee can be brought forward from out of our existence in time. The "border zone" appears to be the area at the horizon. It is there that the pseudo-revelation of reason is called to account. It is there that it appears incapable of being its own judge. All "present thinking" disappears in the amassed thinking of the centuries. Such is the stream of "history." But history is more than all aspects *of* history together. It is set between the Word's Beginning and its judgment that has already started from yonder side of the horizon and that from there will be brought to its fulfillment. Real "knowing" is completely determined by what has been decided by this Judgment, while all supposed knowing is driven in its direction in order to be judged. All rebellious attempts at knowing *are* dynamically *driven* forward, for without reaching for true knowing, no living, not even the poorest and most reduced living, can possibly continue. This reaching-after that leads all of our doing, thinking, and theoretical pursuits is what we call "faith."

Faith is reaching for knowing, for the horizon from which Truth's invitation comes to us. *All* of our experiences, all historical power formation, *all* closure, and *all* refusal begins with faith. For there is no other option than to follow the track of time, for it is meant to serve the disclosure of the Creator's revelation. In other words, all "structures" of human experience, subjective and objective, follow this track of time in the mutual movements of the modalities of experience. This goes on until humankind, in apostasy and liberation, will have exhausted its dynamics, when from "yonder side" the end of temporal "history" is declared.

19. Root and thought

Two more points require our attention. The first concerns the specific nature of theoretical activity. We already dealt with this when discussing the so-called "Gegenstand relation" and its significance for a theory of knowledge. We explained that we could not agree with the supposed necessity of crafting a theory of knowledge first off. The critical investigation of the possibilities of knowing was initiated by Kant in his *Critique of Pure Reason*. His intention in doing so was to safeguard the freedom of "practical Reason" from theoretical attacks. In a similar vein, the Philosophy of the Cosmonomic Idea intended its transcendental critique to fend off attacks on what it called its "religious a priori." This is why transcendental criticism was deliberately made to precede its own theory of structure, even though the structure of theoretical thought

82

would eventually have to be investigated in that theory.

The critical point here is that intentional knowing from out of the root of creation was uncritically endowed with an immanent synthesizing function. (This is similar to the way in which Kant invoked logical judgment in his analysis of what is implicit to the categorical imperative.) Although we agreed with the counter-attack on the cogito etc., we were of the opinion that the theory of knowledge does not deserve the priority given to it here. After all, theoretical thinking is only one *specific* organization of *thinking*. Together with making *practical* distinctions, theoretical thinking functions within *knowing*, which is the responsible root-consciousness of man as taken up in the encompassing creational dynamics.

The uncritical move here is the transition *from* the root of the cosmos *to* the acts of theoretical thinking. Because these are specifically qualified by the logical-analytical modality, they were regarded as acts of thought *par excellence*. But the truth is that they are performed in the coherence of *all* modalities. As we amply demonstrated in *Sign and Motive of Creation* and in *Radix, Time, and Knowing,* there is, on this point, no particular reason to pay special attention to what immanence philosophy has called the "Gegenstand relation."

The Gegenstand relation only becomes important when we have to critically assess the pretensions of immanence philosophy, and then Hegel's distinction between "for us" and "for it" can serve to uncover that pretension with its unclarified meaning. This discovery then teaches us that the specifically theoretical act of thought pertains to the logical-analytical modality. The latter is no more important than other subject-object relations. Claims to the contrary can only appear to have any validity on the standpoint of immanence philosophy. But in reality such priority is an illusion. This claim had its sole ground in the basic religious dialectics of humanism.

With that in mind, and with some reiteration of what came before, we will conclude with a few remarks about the choice of position, both with regard to knowing in the broadest sense and with regard to some more particular ways of knowing.

20. A priori knowing and structural knowing

It is *knowing* in the broad sense that is all-decisive. Without it, there is no horizon awareness, and no responsibility in going through time. Without such knowing there is no way to avoid the antinomies caused by the dynamics of mistaken basic drives. Therefore, without such knowing, there is simply no way in which a direction can be chosen that will lead man, and with him the cosmos itself, to his destination.

We repeat that this knowing is not a special activity of man, besides other activities, still less that it would be some kind of "specialist" knowledge. It is integral, fundamental, decisive. The route of this knowing issues from the root of each individual existence, as this is rooted in the radix of creation.

The particular ways of knowing in the multifariousness of life are only possible because of this original knowing. And they are directed by it. This happens by means of acts and actions. First and primary among these are the acts that pertain to man as man and to his social life; even the "objectifying" acts concerned with nature have always been taken into man's service. This is how it should be. Clearly, the real order here is opposite to its depiction by positivism and materialism. There may be lots of talk about human dignity, neighborly love, and so on and so forth, but used in this way, they can only serve as slogans in the battle for power. But the real order should be taken into account when we design a method or an instrument. We cannot avoid our responsibility here, for the knowing implied in such acts *is* a responsible consciousness of disclosure, whether we want it to or not. Call it "thinking" if you like, if only it is clear that this is no theoretical thinking. It is not even some form of theoretical thinking in the making. What we are concerned with here is the *universality* in its own sphere of logical-analytical insight. It dynamically pervades *all* the acts that we perform.

Theoretical (scientific) *thinking* is merely one of the particular kinds of practical human activity. As such, it is to render its uniquely qualified service. In a certain phase of history its responsibility is to serve humankind as it makes its distinctions via the multiplicity of its variously structured practical acts. Making distinctions has always been and will always remain part of human living; even though, difficult as it is to imagine, systematic theory might at some point in time, by some influence or other, disappear. Conversely, contemporary christian experience has to be vigilant with regard to the confidence placed in science and theoretical thought. For it is in these that modern man celebrates his *cult* of power. It is a matter of *great urgency* that we continually check and re-interpret all "factuality" against the norm of disclosure, first practically and then theoretically.

Our calling as creatures *places* us on the road of knowing. But as soon as we refuse to take the direction indicated by this calling, we inevitably get entangled in the various mutually contradictory options left open for our self-service. For we remain bound to the structures as they have been normatively, that is to say, creationally, *given*. It appears that the choice between true and untrue, between opening and closing, is primarily regulated by our behavior under two modal norms. The first is the one according to which we are to distinguish individuality structures from each other by their "qualifying function." The second is the one that rules all our decisions, namely, *faith*. The historical formation of power is first and foremost dependent upon our subjective choice under these two norms.

For our days, the following question yields a telling example: Will the formative organs within economically qualified relations be satisfied with economic power, or will they attempt to reach beyond that, for example, in order to exercise political power? They will be all the more tempted to do so in the measure that they materialistically regard the economic point of view as determinative of the whole of man's destination. Then, from its side, the state's power of public justice will forsake its own proper qualification and yield to the disclosure dynamics of this same economistic point of view.

We came across another example in the misunderstanding of the qualification of theoretical activity, which led to the age-old error of regarding theoretical thinking as nigh *perfect* thinking, by which theory was promoted to the rank and status of a cult. The structures of the various acts and actions, as they are actualized by the various human societal relations, are fit for man's proper responsibility as it flows from his integral creational responsibility. But when all of life is directed by a temporal destination, the actualization of these structures is distorted in a revolutionary and confusing way, such that true responsibility is in principle counteracted.

By such a course of action, man will in various ways—and in virtually all areas of life—get engulfed by the fog of "the border zone." Consequently, theologians, who have yet to escape from the nature-supernature motive, nowadays reverse the order of their dialectics. Their advice is to—above all else—stay on "this side." And so, with one stroke, this choice disconnects the structures of our life from our life's direction and leaves them completely arbitrary. Should we, in reaction, free ourselves from our responsibility for earthly existence? May we regard the creational earthly journey of faith merely as a perspective along the road towards "yonder side" that has hardly any connection with the goal of our journey?

As we have already explained in various ways, it is not for naught that the journey towards the Fatherland carries us through earthly creation. Even more: We take creation to be the revelation of the reality of this destination. When we discover this, we can take two opposite attitudes. The first one leads to the horizontalistic identification of the earthly journey with "this world." That is what the whole of mankind has done, listening to the whispering of the seducer. Those who make the most effort to deny the "fall," or to water it down, are the ones who most forcefully confirm its devastating reality precisely by their consistent desire to take *control* of creation. The original autonomy-faith of humanism is the most clear demonstration of this. Initially this faith was a matter of investment in modern science, only later to become a raw struggle for power with the aid of science. Now, inside and outside humanism, it is, after the West, taking the whole world down. The quasi-scientific counterarguments of quasi-modern theology are of no avail, for the whole of history confirms what the Word revealed. In this we see the character and the "composition" of revelation demonstrated before our eyes. God's word told us so, fallen creation shows it, but it can only be understood by him whose eyes have been opened by faith. Not a faith in the sense of "accepting," but faith in the sense of deeply lived experience. As it is reflected in the apostle's words: "Who will rescue me from this body that is subject to death?" (Romans 7:24).

We do not have to be surprised by the attempts to weaken faith, nor even by efforts to dispense with it completely. Such efforts come from man, and from theology in the vanguard, in the very same attitude of self-preservation that had led Paul to his exclamation in the first place. But the Word continues to speak: ironically, passionately, cutting deeply, and invitingly. The road *will continue* to lead through creation, supplying me with everything that I need. At the same time, (if I do not defiantly close my eyes) it will continue to teach me in all my travel experiences that it was *my* fall that made the journey painful and dangerous and will continue to do so. Will I be able to take that, or will I want to leave it? At every new mile-post, the horizon looms before me. I can shut my eyes to it, but eventually a time will come when I will have to cross a boundary. And I know that whatever I propose to proclaim about it, either now or then, will remain a powerless uttering.

But there is another option. It is the option of complete surrender. This is what my created being *really* has to tell me. Complete surrender. It means that I desire to disown nothing of what my creatureliness makes me experience. It means that in the growth of my responsible consciousness, in every act and action, I try, with ever increasing effort, to understand its structure as God has intended it. It means that as the world turns I must look forward in two dimensions, knowing that when I am to cross the horizon, the coincidence of these two dimensions will not expire in an eternal nightfall. Complete surrender means that I have heard from afar the calling voice of the Father and that I haste to follow His invitation. Then the meaning of the journey will become clear to me. As the apostle John writes: "When you were younger you dressed yourself and went where you wanted, but . . ." (John 21:18).

A light falls, then, back over my path. Much is demanded from me in the confusing "border zone." Everything, in fact. For the Word that called creation into being has desired to live here. It is here that we have seen his glory, as of the only Son, God's suffering Servant, from whom everyone hid his face, because his suffering could not be looked at. If this has been His "glory," then it is clear to me where mine is. John again: "Then he said to him: 'Follow Me!'" (John 21:19).

Enough has been said. No theologizing about Genesis 1 or Genesis 3. No speculation about counter powers, supposed to have caused "my" fall. No inner mystical wrestling to liberate myself from the bonds of darkness, an impossibility anyway, since it was I myself who was the cause of it. But after the command of Him Who goes on ahead *because* He has fulfilled His purposes, I know that I have to continuously examine all my acts and experience their meaning with my gaze fixed on *Him*, for *that is the meaning of creation*. He who is born of God hears the words of God. That will prove to have been worth the effort. Time for Reflection!

CPSIA information can be obtained at www.ICGtesting.com
Printed in the USA
BVOW07s0733110914

366314BV00001B/181/P